OUT OF THE GHETTO

Out of
the Ghetto

A Path to Socialist Rewards

Mike Prior and Dave Purdy

Spokesman

1000 113 250

First published in 1979 by Spokesman, Bertrand Russell House, Gamble Street, Nottingham NG7 4ET

Cloth ISBN 0 85124 259 6
Paper ISBN 0 85124 246 4

Copyright © Mike Prior and Dave Purdy

Printed by the Russell Press Ltd., Nottingham

Acknowledgements

We have received help and criticism from many people in writing *Out of the Ghetto*. In particular, Steve Bodington, Judith Gray, Katja Hehn, Adah Kay, Phil Leeson, Barry Hindess, Gerry Leversha, Roger Simon, and Ian Steedman gave us advice which was always useful even when we failed to agree. Bill Warren helped us with an earlier draft but died before we finished the final version. Without his early help there is a lot we would never have understood and without his final comments the work is diminished.

Contents

Introduction

It is nearly always possible for contemporary observers to believe that their age is of historic significance, that the choices faced by their society at that moment will determine its future for years to come. And, nearly always, such self-importance can come to seem ridiculous in the light of actual events. New directions for a society seldom occur with the regularity of a railway timetable and social theory, including Marxist theory, has often tended to look for the arrival of old trains rather than the departure of new ones.

Nevertheless this book is written in the belief that the next few years are likely to prove of historic significance for Britain and, in particular, for the left in Britain.

The main basis for this assertion is the precipitate decline in the economic and political status of Britain over the last decade. This needs little in the way of illustration. We discuss the reasons for this decline in some detail below. All that is needed here is one conclusion, that the failure of the Labour administration of 1964-70 even to begin its heralded modernisation of British society marked a watershed in British political life. From the moment of that failure, when the belief that a new direction could be found within the framework of the old system gave way to the usual patch-and-pray ad-hocery, the normal processes of British government began a long-drawn out holding operation, a desperate attempt to hold the centre in the face of mounting centrifugal pressure. That this holding operation has been carried out so smoothly is a testament to the extraordinary resilience and adaptiveness of the British ruling elite and to its powers of consensual domination. Yet it has remained a holding operation for all that; a series of temporary expedients which have held off the more open and dangerous forces.

An on/off incomes policy has just about kept the economic militancy of the unions under control without the rigidities of central pay limits causing too serious a backlash. Commissions, reports, tactical retreats and armed intervention have held the nationalist demands threatening the integrity of the British state. And a combination of bluff and mortgages have produced the international support necessary to prevent the economic problems of Britain escalating to financial disaster.

But neither to these, nor to any of the other problems of British society, have any permanent solutions been found. No new political and social framework has been produced within which these tensions could be eased and reduced to the normal pattern of pressure and counter-pressure, inside some universally accepted (or at least acknowledged) code. And, it must be emphasised, such a framework is required if social development is to proceed by any other path than a series of jumps from crisis to crisis.

The oil-revenues have produced a small and temporary stabilisation of one, but only one, of these incipient crises – the chronic trade deficits which have mounted up whenever the British economy has started to expand. This temporary bulwark may enable the holding operation to be continued for a few years longer. It may also act as the catalytic moment for a wider change. What it cannot do is allow the present system to perpetuate itself for an indefinite period. The crises will recur, not just in the economy but in social integration and political institutions until a solution is found.

Mention of a new social order will no doubt give many socialists two reflex visions – of a fascist dictatorship or a socialist revolution. These are the two outcomes that Marxist theory usually allocates to capitalism in crisis. Whilst the former cannot be ruled out, and there would be no point in this essay if we did not personally believe in at least the possibility of the latter, in reality a much wider range of choices exists. It is not relevant to speculate here on which is the most likely. The point that matters is the existing structural crisis and the necessity for change.

This structural crisis provides half the basis for the assertion of the special importance of the present period. The other half, and the one which is most germane to our purpose, is the current situation of the British left.

The last ten years have been the most important for British socialism since the first decades of this century. In the early 20s, socialist political action and thought froze into a mould which lasted, with few exceptions, for over forty years. Only in the mid-60s did the pattern break with the growth of a new wave of working class militancy accompanied by an array of new political movements amongst women, students, racial minorities and in community action and environmental protection.

The 70s may not have been a 'red decade' in the sense of achieving socialism but it has widened the base of socialist and radical action to a very considerable extent.

The nature of these movements has reflected the nature of the times. They have been, in the most general sense, currents of 'disobedience', in which wide sections of society have refused to accept the roles and the area of manouevre allowed them by bourgeois political rule. Unions, and in particular shop-stewards, have refused to be bound by the unwritten rules of negotiation drawn up in the 50s whereby union power was exerted with implicit restraint in money wage demands, in return for 'responsible' attitudes by employer and government towards industrial relations and employment policy. Women have refused to accept the role of mother, housewife and second-class worker. Communities have refused to accept the decisions of expert planners and students have come to expect some say in their own education.

Such generalised disobedience has enormous significance in developing new forms of struggle and in raising the objective of popular control as a real and attainable demand rather than a far-off utopia. But what cannot be done by such movements, acting alone, is to form their disparate

demands into an alternative vision
acquire the political muscle necessi
this vision. The problem for socialists
that history has presented us with only t\
and theories for this, the narrowly politicä
of socialism, and neither has any great relev. io
the problem we face.

One of them, the Fabian strategy of social
reform, updated by Crosland, is strongly entrenched
in the dominant working class party, the Labour
Party. The other, the Leninist model of Marxism,
is the accepted wisdom of virtually all groups to
the left of the Labour Party and strongly influences
the political philosophy of the traditional Labour
left.

The results of the dominance of these two
models is that the emergence in the 70s of a
political strategy for socialism has been slow and
masked under a variety of verbal disguises. New
and important views within the Labour Party,
generally associated with Benn, have been forced
into a curiously stilted and suppressed frame by the
inability of its main leaders to consider openly the
problems of political power outside the reference
point of the primacy of parliamentary democracy.
Changes within the Communist movement have
been similarily retarded by a need to pay homage
to old gods and hallowed tradition. It has meant
for example, that a Communist party which is
quite clearly *not* Leninist in its strategic perspective
has been unable to come to terms with its retention
of a Leninist mode of organisation.

It is this delay in establishing a central political

purpose which marks out the specific importance of the next few years for British socialism. The gaping holes which have opened in bourgeois domination may yet be closed by some new social order within British capitalism. The positive socialist alternative does not yet exist as a political entity however much progress may have been made in laying its foundations.

This should not be taken as another call for the formation of a new socialist party which could transcend all the mistakes of the old. The organisational problem of the left is unity. That some socialists can seriously regard the formation of any further organisations as a step towards such unity is only a mark of just how serious that problem is. Yet it is also true that unity of the left remains an unrealistic vision, given the dominance of the Leninist and Fabian positions. The very concept of unity between, say, the environmental movement and the trade-unions, remains essentially undefined except on an individual basis of joint involvement.

We are paradoxically in a situation where the richness and diversity of the left has outrun the political concepts that we possess to handle their coordination, mutual support and unification around common political objectives.

In this book, we are trying to explore these concepts and the policies which are needed by the socialist movement to cope with the gap between the social conditions and forces favourable to socialist advance and their political articulation. Starting from certain theoretical abstractions and an analysis of postwar British history, we have tried to argue a political case that is consistent and relevant to the real problems of British social- ism. The fact that we have started from theoretical abstraction means that the first part of the essay is concerned with the elaboration and definition of a theory that some may find obscure and remote from reality. Insofar as this stems from a failure in our powers of clear exposition, some apology is due. But we would defend the general need to start from such a theoretical base.

British political life is not as bereft of theory as is often maintained. A political practice as solidly based as, for example, that of British trade unions cannot function without some firm underlying ideology. The difficulty is that this base is seldom articulated and, more surprisingly, is not often directly considered by a Marxist theory which tends to move within a closed group. We believe that the time is well advanced for concepts such as 'hegemony' to be removed from the arena of Marxist theoreticians and put to some use. The way in which we develop such ideas may well be challenged. To take an example, many socialists will disagree with the conclusions which we draw about incomes policies from our initial assumptions about the need to expand working class hegemony. All we ask is that attacks on our conclusions are devoted either to breaking down our reasoning or to discarding our initial assumptions: our critics should not attempt to have their cake and eat it.

The fact is that many of the theoretical ideas which are common currency on the left have not yet been followed through to their practical implications. And when this is done, it may well be that these implications are hard, and difficult to accept and assimilate. The achievement of a socialist Britain will require the prior transformation of the socialist movement *even* if the transition to socialism is envisaged as a gradual and peaceful process. And that transformation will require hard pounding and not soft words.

It will also require the active involvement of agencies of change and not just the passive acceptance of ideas. One criticism of this essay may be that it remains in the realm of ideas rather being involved with the tactical problems of developing those agencies of change, be they parties, trade unions or other social movement. We can only say that we have gone as far as we are able in spelling out the practical implications of our position. To go further would mean making interventions in areas so detailed and so contingent as to make our comments worthless. We are however fully aware of the need to engage in those practical and flawed bodies which make up the socialist movement.

We have written this piece as a self-contained whole, without references, quotations or acknowledgements save to those who directly criticised our manuscript. This is quite deliberate though it will be obvious that little of what we write is original. It is however difficult to dispel the ghosts of history from any attribution, even when a quote from so-and-so could express a point far more pithily and clearly than our own words. And as for our contemporaries, whose ideas we have freely plundered, all we can do is thank them and offer the same freedom in return. There is a space opening up between the two monoliths and it would be quite wrong to suggest that we have not been preceded and preempted by others. Finally we should thank many unnamed comrades, particularily women, whose bravery, wit and inspiration have showed us that political argument is not incompatible with love and toleration and who started the hard pounding long before our soft words.

The Theoretical Foundations of Socialist Strategy

The purpose of this chapter is to develop some of the theoretical concepts which have shaped and been shaped by our observations on advanced capitalism and on socialist strategy. No attempt is made to provide a comprehensive assessment of Marxist social and political theory. Our concern is to chart a sector of theory which will be used consistently as a guide through the rest of the analysis.

What follows is divided into three sections. In the first we establish the most general concepts which have informed our analysis and explore the much invoked distinction between mode of production and social formation. In the second we investigate the meaning and relevance of Gramsci's concept of hegemony for the analysis of the advanced capitalist countries. In the third we confront the question: what is meant by the term "advanced capitalism"? The answer involves an assessment of the nature of bourgeois democracy and of the significance of the growth of state activitity. At various points in the course of the argument we indicate its general implications for socialist strategy and for the very conception of socialism itself as a state of social existence.

Modes of Production and Social Formation

When we are discussing capitalism — what it is, how it functions, how it has developed — it is essential to distinguish between capitalism as a mode of production and capitalism as an entire social system. The concept of a mode of production refers to any determinate set of social relations within and through which human beings are organised to accomplish the various processes of production and reproduction. One can analyse any mode of production, of which one example is capitalism, in abstraction from any particular country or historical period in which this mode of production has existed. Such abstract analysis is appropriate if the question at issue is for example: what are the principal elements and relationships of the capitalist mode of production? Clearly, however, the answer to this kind of question forms only the starting point for analysing the history of real capitalist social formations, that is, those actual societies in which capitalism has become dominant over other modes of production such as for example, the domestic mode based on the unpaid labour of women in the family or a mode based on independent artisans. To suppose otherwise, to imagine that abstract analysis of a mode of production either eliminates or somehow diminishes the need for concrete analysis of concrete conditions is a form of idealism. Whether in Stalinist, Trotskyist or other manifestations the elevation of the holy abstract over the profane empirical has tended to be associated in practice with dogmatic, elitist and

sectarian attitudes reminiscent of the worst excesses
of religious bigotry.

The concept of a mode of production should
not be understood as being identical with the
economy. The reason is simple. It is impossible to
specify solely in economic terms the relationships
within and through which human beings carry out
the process of material reproduction. The concept
of a mode of production spans the conceptual
space traditionally thought to divide "base" and
"superstructure". As an illustration of this general
point consider the concept of the surplus product.
In Marxist theory, the core of any analysis of the
functioning of a particular mode of production
consists of an account of how a surplus product is
generated, appropriated and utilised. This concept
of surplus product has as its twin the concept of
the necessary costs of reproduction. These are the
costs which have to be provided for out of what is
produced, if production is to continue on an
undiminished scale. The surplus is, by definition,
a surplus with respect to these costs.

In the most simplified account of how a given
mode of production works, these necessary costs
can be reduced to just two items: replacement
of whatever physical inputs are used up in the
processes of production plus the provision of some
level of "subsistence" to the direct producers.
But it is immediately obvious that no system of
production could successfully perpetuate itself
without many other conditions being satisfied
besides these two. For instance, some minimum
degree of law and order must prevail, in the sense

that the general function of preserving law and order has to be performed somehow, the precise institutional form depending on the mode of production in question. But legal institutions belong indisputably to the political and ideological levels of the social structure. The law punishes, deters, regulates conflicts, constitutes social practices such as marriage and contracts, prescribes certain codes of conduct and so on.

It is thus apparent that no mode of production can be neatly comparmentalised within the economy. This in turn means that it is misleading to depict the three levels of the social structure which Marxists normally distinguish — the economic, the political and the ideological — as resting on top of each other like the storeys of a building with the implication that the upper tiers could somehow be removed to leave an intact economic base in full working order. It is sometimes analytically convenient to confine attention to just one of these levels at a time, leaving the others in the background. Marx did this for most of the time in *Capital*. But, as Marx was aware, in reality none can subsist independently of the others. All are jointly necessary to the constitution of a mode of production, though the way they interlock differs from one mode to another.

The most important reason why abstract analysis of a mode of production is insufficient to understand any actual society is that no single mode of production has ever embraced all the processes of material production in any actual historic society. The social formations of antiquity contained pockets of capitalist, petty commodity production and peasant agriculture alongside the prevailing systems of slavery. Slavery in its turn persisted through the Middle Ages as the extreme point of a spectrum containing the manorial serf system, forms of indentured labour and artisan production. In the non-slave-owning states of North America, which left their feudal antecedents behind in Europe, subsistence and petty commodity production retained a substantial hold alongside capitalism even in the late nineteenth century. In short, real social formations always combine diverse modes of production.

Not that it is sufficient to characterise a social formation simply by listing its various modes of production. These are not strung together like charms on a necklace. One has to show concretely how they are related to, depend on and interact with each other. This is a demanding task because diverse modes interpenetrate to produce particular adaptations and mutant social forms. It is this interpenetration of modes which gives any society its specific historic character. Characterisations of a society as "late" this or "early" that ignore this point by suggesting that historical change occurs through some process of unilateral maturation.

Normally one mode of production can be identified as dominant. Contemporary Britain, for example, can be identified as a capitalist economy. Precisely what this means is easier to see in concrete applications than in terms of a general definition. Indeed the concept of the dominant mode of production positively requires to be set to work in concrete analysis before its value can be realised. In the abstract it is a mere promise awaiting fulfilment, a feature which it shares in common with other Marxist concepts like hegemony, balance of forces, dominant class and so on.

Dominance is certainly not a matter of quantitative presence, though that can be important. A relatively small area of capitalism, for example, can exert a force for change out of all proportion to its quantitative weight. The same is true for an emergent socialist mode of production. The conquest of the commanding heights of the economy need not be synonymous with the nationalisation of every large enterprise, if those concerns under national control serve to direct and focus the remaining firms in the private sector. Equally, comprehensive nationalisation may preserve and strengthen characteristically capitalist social forms and relations with respect, say, to the hierarchy of control, the interpersonal division of labour or social accountability. It is, therefore, important to analyse the balance between dominant and subordinate modes on *all* levels of the social formation and to recognise that the scales may be differently inclined at each level. Thus, to assert that the capitalist mode of production is dominant within contemporary Britain is no more than a shorthand summation of a complex series of statements. As far as the economy is concerned it means that a substantial (though by certain criteria, e.g. share of total employment, a minority) sector of economic life which is directly organised under capitalist relations of production, supplies the economy's main, though not exclusive, dynamic. Amonst other things, this means that decisions and actions taken within this sector exert the major influence on such key issues as the timing, volume, pattern and location of investment or the scale and composition of overseas trade. Ideologically, capitalist dominance implies that certain characteristically capitalist social practices and the outlook on life which expresses and sustains these practices, are deeply ingrained into the texture of social life. As a result of the various socialisation processes which they experience and their daily participation in "the capitalist way of life" people tend to acquire such attitudes as individualism, acquiescence in expertise, acquisitiveness, and so on. At the political level, capitalist dominance means that the processes of policy formation and the main political conflicts occur largely within limits which take for granted the economic and social balances of capitalism. It also means that the myriad problems and issues which are thrown up by the march of events can be more or less successfully resolved within these limits.

The balancing analogy which was used above suggests a crucial and largely neglected feature of the relationship between dominant and subordinate modes of production. The dominance of capitalist relations of production within capitalist social formations is not an immutable, pre-given condition which is always automatically assured outside of moments of extreme crisis. It is not true that a society is solidly capitalist until some revolutionary epoch when it changes to socialism, just as it is not true that feudalism passed into capitalism in a smooth, steady evolution without conflict and without the eventual outcome of that conflict being uncertain. The balance between modes of production is always liable to alteration. In certain conditions the scales can be tilted against capitalism without a violent rupture within the political system. By the same token they may be tilted back again.

An example of such a shift and its reversal is the course of events in Britain during and after the Second World War. For the duration of the war Britain was placed on a footing which, although not socialist, had strong elements of that social collectivism which is at least part of socialism. The means of production were not taken into public ownership on any widespread scale. But the principles guiding social action had a strong egalitarian and collectivist flavour. By deliberately suppressing competitive market forces the state placed the capitalist economy in a condition of suspended animation. After the war there ensued a protracted conflict between the incipient socialism contained within this social collectivism and the traditional capitalist principles of free enterprise, individualism and laissez-faire. In the class compromise, by which this clash was temporarily resolved, socialist gains were not annulled. But their further expansion received a check. Elements of socialism — embodied in the welfare state, the commitment to macro-economic management and a full employment policy and the nationalisation of key sectors — were integrated into a new social equilibrium in which capitalism retained its overall dominance.

We must emphasis that we are not suggesting that 'islands' of socialism exist within a capitalist Britain. Socialism is represented within these areas as a set of socialising factors which tend to work towards a future socialist society, and away from the present capitalism. They conflict and, normally, are contained by those factors which act to preserve capitalism. Within the health service, the ideological factor of providing free service to all patients is in conflict with the constraints of elitist medical practice, non-democratic control and arbitrary financial constraint. But the conflict is real and represents a conflict between factors arising out of a mixed mode of production.

This notion of an ongoing conflict between structurally antagonistic modes of production co-existing within the same social formation is crucial to the subsequent argument. It is also necessary to be clear that the dominant mode of production is not identical with the progressive mode of production. The dominant mode may lack the capacity to resolve the major social and economic issues of the day from within its own resources. In order to sustain itself and to integrate both individual and social needs at various levels of society into a stable synthesis it may have to rely on partial and contradictory borrowings from outside itself.

The previous example of postwar Britain illustrates how British capitalism was enabled to survive and even, by the standards of its own historical past, to flourish, by incorporating some of the dynamics of socialism. It is this phenomenon, the pre-emptive borrowing of elements of the class enemy's programme in order to forestall revolution, for which Gramsci coined the phrase "passive revolution". The borrowed elements do not, however, become totally submerged. They do not completely lose their progressive character by virtue of being harnessed to the dominant mode. Because they derive ultimately from an antagonistic mode of production they always retain a threatening potential and remain a continuing focus of political and ideological conflict. It is hard to see how the experience of the UK since the onset of acute economic crisis in 1973-4 can be understood in any other terms. On every front of economic and social policy, from the control of the national health service to the control of the money supply, the most fundamental principles of social organisation and action have been locked in combat. That this combat has been fought out in the idiom of reform rather than revolution should not obscure its importance.

The implications of this point for left political practice are pursued further later. For the moment we simply wish to stress that a nascent, progressive mode of production which is subordinated to the dominant mode, has a twofold nature. It serves both to sustain and to deform the dominant mode. Provided this point is correctly grasped gains which have been realised through passive revolution can become vantage points for further advance.

A general example of this is nationalisation of manufacturing industries. This has been adopted by the governments of most capitalist countries as a means of coping with the social and political problems of declining industries or with economic recession. The immediate result of nationalisation is usually to stabilise capitalism by removing sources of social unrest or by containing economic problems within some small industrial sector. The long term results of nationalisation depend upon a wide range of factors: the position of the national-ised sector within the economy, the attitudes of the workforce, the general level of socialist mobil-isation and so on. However the fact that an industry has been removed from the confines of market forces, and this remains the fundamental if some-times disguised feature of nationalised industries, always *tends* to force that industry towards social involvements which private industry would avoid.

A government may choose to allow a particular industry to conform to market forces, but it is a choice and not an unalterable condition. This may or may not assist the political development of socialism and it is clear that precipitate and large scale nationalisation can sometimes strengthen rather than weaken capitalism. But the appreciation of the balance of forces in any particular moment can only be made by understanding the process that is occurring; the constant attempts at absorp-tion of socialist forms, and the countering re-generation and vitalising of elements of socialism, within a capitalist economy.

The distinction made between mode of pro-duction and social formation highlights the com-plexity of social reality. The nature of a social formation cannot be distilled down into some all pervasive principle or essence. When we are investigating the structure or history of a particular social system there is no escaping from the necessity for concrete analysis. Abstract analysis can point us in the right general direction, but it cannot decide the route to be travelled in advance of the journey. It can, for example, elucidate the sources and nature of the principal class conflicts within capitalism. This provides a rough set of bearings for political practice, but no more. It does not offer a handbook catering for all the possible configurations of social forces which may make an appearance in history. Real historically lived struggles are always "imperfect". Political and cultural forces emerge which do not neatly reflect economic class interests. The fundamental social classes may be fragmented along religious, ethnic, territorial, economic-functional or other lines. Inter-class relations may be overlaid by intra-class conflicts and divisions.

If fundamental class antagonisms were not refracted in this way, both the task of maintaining and the task of replacing a given social order would become enormously simplified. In the last analysis the outcome of class struggle would depend not on which class showed the greater constructive capacity for resolving social and economic problems, but on which side showed the greater destructive ability to defeat its opponent in physical combat.

Few Marxists would ever admit to such a crude, one-dimensional view of capitalism. But the political practice of Marxist groups has often implied some such conception. Thus the economic struggle of the working class in its capacity as owner and trader of labour power is sometimes regarded as the only authentic form of class struggle. Struggles on other fronts or involving non-working class groups are dismissed as irrelevant or divisive. Alternatively, they are treated as optional extras, welcome, but dispensable additions to the "real" forces. Or finally, even if issues such as national independence, racial and sexual liberation, the protection of the environment, the rights of children, youth and old age, or the re-habilitation of residential communities are conceded validity in their own right, as necessary extras, they are subordinated to what is deemed to be the central arena of struggle over the terms on which labour power is bought and used by capital.

This is not to argue for an approach to politics which simply picks up all points of social conflict as being of equal importance. The point is that what kinds of social and political advance are possible and what combinations of forces can be expected to realise such advance can only be determined by concrete analysis, not by a priori decree.

The Concept of Hegemony

The insights into the nature and sources of class domination in the advanced capitalist states, which we owe to the fecund, but cryptic, writings of Gramsci, are now part of the conventional wisdom of the left. Gramsci's essentially new concept was that of hegemony, which he developed well beyond the restricted meaning attached to the term by Lenin and the theorists of the Second International. Hegemony in Gramsci's sense refers to a mode of domination by one class or section of a class over other social classes and groups, which rests predominantly on consent as opposed to coercion or violence. Such consent may be passively enjoyed or actively cultivated by the dominant group, but in both cases if subordinate social groups either tacitly accept or positively endorse the prevailing social order, the dominant group is said to possess hegemony over them.

The success and survival of the dominant group depends on both power secured by coercion and power derived from consent. Both these modes of power are intertwined in the institutions which make up a particular social formation, though their relative weight varies across different institutions. Gramsci sometimes sought to register this variation by drawing a distinction between "the state" or "political society" and "civil society", though his usage of these terms was not always consistent. Thus he sometimes defined the state narrowly to include only those agencies whose functions are primarily co-ercive and which possess a monopoly of legitimate violence, whereas "civil society" embraces all those institutions which serve to construct and reproduce consent to the established social order. The proliferation and growth of state activity in contemporary capitalism together with the allied advance of bourgeois democracy, both geographically and institutionally, beyond the stage it had reached in Gramsci's day, render this particular usage anachronistic and misleading. Gramsci's abiding contribution, now so belatedly applauded, lies in his recognition of the preponderant role of consent in the advanced capitalist countries and in his pioneering exploration of the implications of this condition for socialist strategy in these states.

What is perhaps less well understood is that hegemony is not a purely cultural relationship. It is true that many of Gramsci's statements may be given a "culturalist" interpretation. In his writings on intellectuals Gramsci comes near to depicting them as the cerebral craftsmen of a particular social class. They are said to articulate the interests and outlook of that class in writings and pronouncements which are then filtered down amongst the people at large. But whilst intellectual leadership is undoubtedly part of the concept of hegemony it does not tell the whole story. If all that hegemony involved were the elaboration of principles of action by intellectuals and their acceptance by masses of people, then the struggle for hegemony would become one of pure cultural contestation. Its proper sphere would be confined to publications, conferences, education and so on, adding another discrete aspect to the economic class struggle.

Such an essentially educative view of hegemony is one sided and fails to do justice to its material base. Hegemony does have its active side. It does require moral, intellectual and political leadership. But it is necessary to emphasise the passive, spontaneous side of consent formation.

This aspect of hegemony grows out of the entire network of social practices which constitute society. Social institutions such as the electoral and party political systems, collective bargaining and trade unions, the education, health and other public services, modes of transport, recreation and leisure, the family and so on, embody certain definite principles of social action. Through their daily involvement in these practices people tend to become habituated to them. They learn to act according to their defining principles. They acquire a certain set of values, assumptions, expectations. Social being, as Marx put it, determines social consciousness. (Though, it must be added, in a much more complex fashion than is often appreciated by many Marxists).

If existing social practice serves to reproduce the class system and to renew the power of the dominant class, then this class enjoys the support of an organic system of consent generation. By the same token, if this social practice embodies principles of action which anticipate an alternative social order, the hegemony of an erstwhile dominant group may be qualified, suspended or superseded.

As an illustration of the way in which passive hegemony may be disturbed in a particular area of social life, consider the rapid growth and professionalisation of social work since its separation from the health service in the late 1960s. Whatever its other consequences this development has served to highlight the need for the community to take responsibility for coping with "individual" problems such as mental or physical handicap or juvenile delinquency. These are problems which previously were either not recognised as such, or were left for individuals to cope with as best they could, or were handled in a brutalised and authoritarian way. Seen from this standpoint the modern social worker is a carrier of collectivist values which are alien to the standards of capitalism. Increased employment of men in this occupation, and the associated rise in its relative pay and status also help to erode the sexist view that care of dependents is women's work.

That social workers are appointed and paid for by a state committed to the preservation of capitalism is an illustration, on the social level, of the process referred to above of passive revolution. The state in modern capitalism can no longer treat social problems of deprivation as individual examples of profligacy or bad-luck, to be remedied by charity or the workhouse. The maintenance of capitalist hegemony demands that the state intervene to remedy problems that are now seen as arising from the functioning of the system rather than individual chance. Yet the introduction of collective social responsibilities brings about its own dislocations in the structure of capitalism. This constant change in the areas of conflict is characteristic of modern capitalism and reflects the dominant role played by the formation of consent.

The fact that a considerable part of the process of consent formation (or deformation) has this passive character, carries with it two important consequences. The first is that if bourgeois ideas hold sway in society at large this cannot be solely due to bourgeois monopoly and manipulation of the mass media. Bourgeois ideology is not a fraud perpetrated by clever illusionists. The second is that the ideological dominance of a ruling class is unlikely to be total. There are always breaks and discontinuities. The complex of practices which makes up the capitalist way of life determines only the dominant side of people's experience. There remains an underside which is normally repressed, latent or confined to a subterranean existence, but which occasionally breaks through to the surface. This is the reason why exotic, deviant, marginal or simply atypical social phenomena can often reveal more about the nature of social relations than what is considered normal. The normal comes to be so far taken for granted that its preconditions fail to be questioned and investigated.

Thus the appearance of extreme religious sects in Britain in the first half of the 17th century, or the flourishing of alternative sexual lifestyles at the end of the 1960s may have been confined to small minorities and shunned by most 'upright' citizens. But these groups reflected social tensions which were present throughout society even among those whose beliefs and lifestyle were most firmly rejected by the extreme minority. Moreover, these tensions may be important precursors to substantial social and political change.

We have established that the structures of hegemony equip the ruling class with a rich fund of moral capital on which to fall back should its economic or political fortunes falter. But this moral capital is a finite asset. Like the physical capital stock, if it is not from time to time renewed and refashioned it wears out and becomes obsolete. Class rule is not sacrosanct. At certain junctures it must be actively safeguarded and promoted or risk degeneration. The ability to respond creatively to social and economic problems constitutes the active side of hegemony. A system of social defence mechanisms which have grown deep roots over a long period of time, certainly provides a stable foundation for class domination. Without them a dominant group would rest precariously on coercion alone. But stability can only afford protection against disturbance. It does not impose direction. Direction or leadership is a matter of conscious political choice out of what are seen as the available options at any given moment. This is something which no class automatically possesses. It has to be constantly recreated. There is, however, an inherent difficulty for the renovation of bourgeois class leadership in advanced capitalism. It stems from the tensions present in the process of passive revolution discussed earlier. The plagiarising of certain socialist themes in order to regularise the processes of production and reproduction inevitably disturbs the traditional images held and projected by the political and ideological leaders of the ruling class. There is a diminishing area of characteristically bourgeois ideology on which they can rely. Over the long run the result is an ideological crisis. The clearest expression of this at the political level is the continuing vacillation of the Conservative Party between an outdated philosophy of individual self-help and a diluted social collectivism.

Although hegemony can be eroded if it is not periodically revitalised, such a process of internal decay does not necessarily benefit the progressive forces. Social disintegration and regress are always a possibility. The struggle for socialist hegemony can only be waged by an active presence within or alongside the social practices through which hegemony is generated. These practices must be reconstructed in order to destroy the basis for the reproduction of bourgeois ideology and in order to build the cradle in which socialist standards can grow. This active presence may take a variety of forms depending on the nature of the society in question, the degree of physical repression and the historical development of democracy. But in all situations socialism must be a concrete force, limited to propagandistic intervention only when it is compelled to be, but wherever possible embodied in real social institutions and actively changing people's lives.

This active construction of socialism within capitalism does not mean a reversion to the utopian communities of the nineteenth century, though the left needs to show far more sympathy than in the past to their modern equivalents — counter cultures, alternative technologies and life-style politics. These are merely the fringes of a terrain of battle which extends across the entire social formation from the struggles of women to affirm the right of control over their own bodies to the struggles of workers to extend control over their own workplaces, from the neighbourhood health centre up to the highest organs of the state.

What is being projected here is not a sophisticated latter day version of the integrative, consciousness-raising role laid down by Lenin for the revolutionary party in *What is to be done?* It is not a question of a revolutionary party bringing socialist conscious-ness from the outside to struggles which would otherwise remain struggles *within* capitalism rather than against it. What we mean by "socialist consciousness" does not exist in a disembodied, ethereal state attainable only by committed revolutionaries who are "in the know". The process which socialists call "raising the level of consciousness" should be one of apprehending progressive trends and forces which already enjoy a purchase within the existing social order, forging links between diverse struggles and thus amplifying and redirecting their force. This means unlocking the socialist potential lodged within current social practice in order to inscribe its logic firmly into the functioning of society. Viewed in this way socialism is less a distant goal still to be achieved and more a partially achieved reality in the process of formation. Not that there is any inevitability about the outcome of the process. Gains once made can always be lost again, and will be so lost if there is no real appreciation of their significance or no force to defend them against attack.

No doubt there will be many who are inclined to dismiss our conception of the contemporary socialist project in the advanced bourgeois democracies as reformist. For our part we are less interested in name calling than in the substantive question whether our interpretation is coherent and adequate. For the record, however, it is worth noting four major respects in which our perspective departs from classical reformism. First, we do not regard the sole object of social reform as the improvement of the conditions of the people. Reforms are important in their own right but also because of their possible ulterior consequences in unbalancing the defence mechanisms of capitalism.

Second, the agent of social change is not in our view a benign central government enacting progressive legislation on behalf of social groups whose sole function is to offer up loyal electoral support. The state is not a neutral body but an apparatus whose normal purpose is to perpetuate existing class relationships. Our divergence from classic Marxism does not lie in denying its inbuilt bias to support capitalism, but in emphasing the inherent social, ideological, and political contradictions which emerge from the attempt by the state to preserve capitalist hegemony. State action can thus come to play a very ambiguous role in the development of socialist struggle, as it is very often just these contradictions which can give the most leverage within society to progressive forces. But this does not imply in any way that socialism will be achieved by any simple acceleration of progressive state actions. We take literally the conception of socialist transition as popular self-emancipation.

Third, we reject what the early Fabians called

the strategy of permeation. It is true that the Fabians believed that history was on their side and that liberal capitalism was no more than an anarchic interlude between feudal and collectivist forms of social regulation. But their politics consisted essentially of winning over political leaders and opinion-makers by appeals to reason, goodwill or a sense of justice. Marxist politics by contrast aims at a precise specification of the social forces which on the one hand have an interest in particular kinds of social change, and on the other hand have the capacity to achieve them. Once the elements of such a bloc of forces have been identified, the task is one of realising their unity in practice.

Fourth, although we adhere to a conception of the transition to socialism in the advanced capitalist countries as a gradual process rather than a single violent upheaval, we do not deny the likelihood of severe political crises along the way. These crises are not certain to be resolved in favour of socialism. This will happen only to the extent that mass mobilisation in support of socialist policies is a major component of Marxist political action, and that the mechanism for such mobilisation is built into all socialist organisation.

Advanced Capitalism

The previous sections have dealth with (a) contradictions between rival modes of production co-existing within a given social formation; and (b) how the concept of hegemony can illuminate the conditions in which a particular mode of production succeeds or fails in establishing and maintaining its dominance. The conclusions we have reached enable us to come to grips with the question: What does it mean to describe contemporary capitalism as advanced?

It is at once obvious that this question cannot be answered by reference to conventional indices of the development of the productive forces such as the relative proportions of manufacture, agriculture and extraction and services, the level of labour productivity, the size of productive units, patterns of consumption, the degree of urbanisation or the degree of internationalisation of economic and social life. The characteristics of all these measures of development are (1) that they are largely economic; and (2) with due allowance for historical discontinuity they merely mark off successive points in a steady evolution. They do not enable us to specify what it is about contemporary capitalism that justifies the label "advanced" or, for that matter, the adjective "late", which some writers prefer.

The crux of the matter lies in three intertwined historical processes: the maturation of capitalism's political and ideological structures; the consolidation of bourgeois democracy; and the transformation of the role of the state.

1. The Social Reproduction of Capitalism

The "advanced" nature of capitalism lies first in the fact that the complex of social practices through which capitalist social relations are reproduced has grown rich, diverse and solid. This does not mean that violence has been eliminated as an element of social control. The technical gap in means of repression between rulers and ruled is probably wider now than ever before. But the significance of this fact for political strategy can only be assessed in the context of the political and cultural influences which determined the ability and willingness of a dominant class to deploy instruments of violence. It may be argued that violence still remains the determinant basis of class power in the last instance, even if the actual medium through which class power is normally exercised consists of the institutional organisation of mass consent. But this proposition offers precious little tactical and strategic guidance if the mediating instances of politics and ideology indefinitely postpone the lonely hour of the last instance. It is as mistaken to collapse political strategy into preparation for military confrontation as it is to exclude the possibility of violent reaction altogether. Between these extremes strategy can only be based on probabilistic judgement informed by sober analysis of historical experience.

In general the use of violence in advanced capitalism is heavily constrained. It is compelled to operate under a much more detailed set of legitimations than in earlier periods of capitalism. Then the mere demonstration of collective activity by the working class was regarded as a sufficient justification for unleashing coercion. Now particular justifications must be found. Either some general state of social disorder must prevail or certain defined special circumstances are invoked as in the case of the use of psychiatric treatment for "social deviants" in the name of medical science and responsibility. There are gaps and grey areas in the field of legitimation as with the current state of custom and law governing picketing in industrial disputes in Britain. And it goes without saying that the frontiers of legitimate coercive action are the focus of continuous struggle. But capitalism has come to rely more and more heavily on the adequacy of its system of social reproduction.

It is instructive to recall the situation of the working class in Britain in the early part of the nineteenth century. It was not enfranchised. The emergent craft based trade unions were struggling for survival against the hostility of employer and state. Political parties existed only in the most attenuated sense as cliques of magnates with no mass organisation behind them. Neither Tories, Whigs, nor Radicals were organically linked with the working class. Public education, provision for health care, transport and communications were primitive. The mass media in the modern sense did not exist and a large section of the population was illiterate. In short, the working class was effectively excluded from the bourgeois polity.

Moreover, this was a period when fully fledged industrial capitalism based on factory production and a detailed division of labour under the direct control of the capitalist, was only just beginning to emerge. The two largest occupational classes in 1851 were domestic servants and agricultural labourers. Capitalist relations of production were still novel. People had not grown accustomed to them.

The subsequent development of capitalism in Britain transformed these conditions. The change was not smooth — social development rarely is — though there were no cataclysmic interruptions of the sort that occurred in Germany and elsewhere. Industrial capital extended its sway. Its labour processes and relations of production became typical. At a much earlier date than elsewhere the working class became the largest single class. Successive extensions of the franchise opened the way to genuine mass politics with nationally organised political parties, mass circulation newspapers and a vigorous and efficient system of local government. The defenders of capitalism had to learn the politics of the people. Institutions such as universal suffrage, collective bargaining, the freedom to strike, which had previously been identified with revolution, were shown to be compatible with, and even necessary, for the preservation of the social order. Popular pressure for reform and original ruling class initiative combined to create a full grown and stable bourgeois pattern of social life.

2. *The Development of Bourgeois Democracy*

The most obvious and important expression of this sophistication and naturalisation of capitalist social relations has been the development of bourgeois democracy. The term is used here in its conventional sense to include a representative assembly elected periodically on the basis of universal adult suffrage, a plurality of mass political parties, the rule of law together with more or less secure civil liberties, the nominal equality of citizens before the law, the selection of state officials on the basis of merit, the independence of the judiciary and the subordination of military and police forces to civil control. From a long term historical standpoint bourgeois democracy is not simply one of several possible political systems which are all compatible with capitalism. This would imply a purely contingent connection between the bourgeois class and bourgeois democracy. If this were all it amounted to, democracy could be summarily dispensed with whenever the bourgeoisie faced a serious threat. It would be a fair weather system to the fate of which the ruling class was ultimately indifferent.

The destruction of feudal absolutism, the long struggle for religious and civil freedom and the extension of the franchise to a successively larger fraction of the people, represented the modernising and progressive side of capitalist development. Indeed it is sometimes forgotten now that until the mid-nineteenth century "democracy" was a revolutionary or at least a radical term. Certainly one stream of the Marxist tradition does admit the liberating force of the ascendant bourgeoisie. But the bourgeoisie is deemed to have become reactionary once the working class and socialist movement appeared on the scene in the second half of the nineteenth century.

This traditional view is untenable. If true it would imply that the bourgeoisie was perpetually on the brink of imposing some authoritarian system of government and was restrained only by the vigilance and force of the masses. This denies the bourgeoisie any interest of its own in the maintenance and development of bourgeois democracy. Yet by any criterion the kind of parliamentary democracy achieved in Britain has proved to be an enormously flexible and successful system for mediating between classes and adjusting to the problems of preserving the dominance of capitalism. It is altogether unintelligible why the bourgeoisie should undertake the risks of abandoning such a well tried political system.

The experience of fascism in Central, Eastern and Southern Europe between the wars in no way contradicts this view. The conditions in which fascism took root in these countries, included the relative political weakness of the bourgeois class and the corresponding absence of a strong, democratic tradition. It is also significant that the fascists were assiduous in their attention to popular mobilisation and the institutions of civil society. This was the homage paid by fascist vice to bourgeois democratic virtue. Moreover, despite many vacillations, the democratic states did eventually embark on total war with fascism and were prepared to ally with the USSR for this purpose. Doubtless the war aims of the Western Allies were complex and included the weakening of Soviet socialism as well as the defeat of the Axis powers. Nevertheless the war was a critical test of both ruling class and popular allegiance to bourgeois democracy. The success with which capitalism was reconstructed in the defeated powers after the war within a democratic framework testifies to the strength of this allegiance. Far from withering away, the force of attraction exerted by the long run democratic tendency of capitalism can be seen at work in the unheavals of the early 1970s in the Iberian peninsula and Greece, and in the political crises in Italy.

The term "bourgeois democracy" is in any case by now misleading as a description of the political system which has evolved in most of the advanced capitalist states, and particularly in Britain. It suggests a political regime fashioned exclusively in the image and interests of the bourgeoisie. This ignores the degree to which the working class movement has been able to impose its stamp on the system, through the wide and highly ramified layers of institutions which surround and focus on Parliament and Government. Through political parties, through such "extra Parliamentary" organisations as trade unions, in local government, and public committees in areas such as health and education, by representation on and access to official commissions and inquiries, community organisations and an endless variety of pressure groups and campaigns; in all these ways working class influence is brought to bear on the system of government. It defies credibility to deny that any effective influence is exerted through such channels. They would fall into disuse eventually if they yielded no practical payoff.

The normal Marxist response to this massive accumulation of ways of influence is that they all represent co-option or incorporation and that they can only function within the limits of capitalism. This is of course automatically proven, if the criteria for non-co-option and non-incorporation are set at levels which require socialists to work in a manner which is entirely external to the whole system. In any particular sense, the development of even the smallest degree of political influence requires that this complex network of political bargaining is entered and, moreover, that it is used effectively and positively. Any suggestion that a particular individual or group is using established negotiating procedures (which is all these are) in a negative or destructive fashion is a certain route to losing working class support.

In fact, most socialists do accept the need to work within the system. The problem is that, in the absence of any clear theoretical grasp of the function of such work and how it fits in with a revolutionary perspective, the main defence against incorporation is reduced to 'personal integrity' or the generalised moral effects of belonging to the correct political group.

The second objection, to insist that influence can only be applied within the limits of capitalist dominance is a less profound observation than most Marxists seem to believe. What are these limits? What in any case is the ruling class likely to be able or willing to do if these limits are over-stepped? Bourgeois supremacy, as we have argued before, is not guaranteed by some mysterious inner secret of the system. In a democracy especially, it exists in an uneasy tension with the forces and aspiration of other classes and class fractions.

In Britain in particular, the political system in the extended sense used here has been the site of profound social struggle which has visibly affected the allocation of resources and the course of history. Nor is there much evidence for the mechanistic view sometimes canvassed on the left that the scope for significant social reform has been removed with the demise of British imperialism. For example, since 1963 there have been no less than ten major pieces of legislation which have included as a major objective the extension of the rights of trade unions and/or of the individual worker. (The Contracts of Employment Act 1963; the Industrial Training Act 1964; the Trade Union Act 1965; the Redundancy Payments Act 1965; the Equal Pay Act 1970; the Trade Union and Labour Relations Act 1974; the Sex Discrimination Act 1975; the Employment Protection Act 1975 which amongst other things retained the unfair dismissals provisions of the otherwise unloved Industrial Relations Act 1971; the Health and Safety Act, 1974).

These positive features of bourgeois democracy — its resilience and flexibility and the scope it offers for social advance have important implications for socialist strategy. The classical socialist position was defined by the Second International in the period before 1914. This declared that bourgeois democracy should be defended by the socialist movement, or fought for where it did not yet exist, because it afforded the best possible terrain on which the working class could prepare itself for the eventual overthrow of capitalism. Later, the Communist movement evolved a tough minded, suspicious attitude towards democracy based on the practice of the Russian Bolsheviks in the extreme conditions of economic collapse, armed foreign intervention and civil war. For an entire epoch the predominant attitudes on the Marxist left were shaped by the experience of a country where no democratic tradition had ever taken root.

We can now however, begin to appreciate that not only because bourgeois democracy is deeply entrenched in the West, but also because it embodies genuine social advance or the potential for such advance, socialist policies must cut with its grain not against it. This is not a question of tactics but of strategic disposition. Nor does it entail a narrow, electioneering approach to politics. This would be to stop well inside the frontiers of our existing democratic system, which, as we have argued, extends beyond the formal mechanisms of Parliamentary elections. What it does mean is that any perspective of totally abolishing the Parliamentary system, outlawing opposition parties, violating civil liberties and so on, and of substituting for all these a system of "proletarian democracy" is neither feasible, necessary nor desirable.

3. *The Role of the State in Advanced Capitalism*

Linked with the gradual consolidation of bourgeois democracy has been the growth of state involvement in and responsibility for the functioning of the economy and for those facets of social life most closely implicated with the economy. It would be an oversimplification to present state intervention as a direct response to popular pressure. Many of the problems to which state intervention has been applied as a solution were the product of certain long-term tendencies of capitalist development — for example, the various collective issues raised by the process of urbanisation, or the imperatives of rivalry between the main imperialist powers. Similarly the greatest single impulse behind the growth of state intervention in the economy in this century has been war and pre-parations for war. The stimulus which war gives to planning owes much of its force to the total character of modern warfare waged by society as a whole rather than professional armies. A system of large scale planning reaching cumulatively back into the economy and society becomes indispensable as a condition of victory.

We are not here concerned to trace the historical development of state economic intervention, but to evaluate its significance for our investigation into the nature of advanced capitalism. For whatever the causal processes at work and whether state intervention has been primarily motivated by the need to preserve social and political equilibrium or by a desire to develop the productive forces, the common feature persisting through all the modes and varieties of state intervention has been the conscious use of state power to achieve greater control over specific aspects of the functioning of the economy. In this sense there has been a progressive encroachment of the principle of conscious social regulation over the anarchy of capitalist commodity production. Competition has been modified, subdued and in some cases abolished altogether as a principle of economic regulation. Significant elements of competitive anarchy remain. But however important they are, the degree to which the British economy already contains a major degree of regulation should not be forgotten. In a purely economic sense there is little novelty about socialism in Britain.

We do not propose to develop a full treatment of state intervention in advanced capitalism. We consider the issue in a British context later.

Here the role of demand management will serve as an illustration. All countries since the war have utilised taxation, public expenditure, control of credit and the money supply, welfare payments and other aspects of fiscal and monetary policy, including resort to deficit spending, for the purpose of economic stabilisation. Policies have not taken the form of emergency rescue action envisaged by Keynes in the 1930s. They have been used for a variety of objectives – to assist the containment of inflation, to equilibrate the balance of payments, to influence the level of employment (both upwards and downwards), and, in the mid 1970s as bargaining counters in the complex tug of war over resources between the state, capital, the working class and overseas producers of primary commodities.

Demand management has had its critics, mostly on the right. Some have argued that it has been destabilising. Certainly control has been imperfect. But what is important is that the modern capitalist state possesses both the means and the ability to influence aggregate expenditure, if only because it accounts directly for a large proportion of such expenditure. Whether it always chooses to exercise this power is another matter. But in principle it is always possible for the state to affect the level of economic activity in order to achieve some policy target, even if the need to do so arises from an earlier mistake in state policy.

It is also claimed that demand management is now obsolete. This is part of a current fad for debunking Keynesian economics. Amongst right wing devotees it reflects a reactionary and ultimately utopian desire to roll back the frontiers of state intervention. It is also fundamentally anti-democratic. The monetarists' desire that the money supply should be raised each year by an invariable percentage in order to forestall government interference, is, consciously or not, an attempt to take a vital instrument of economic policy out of politics and to insulate it against popular influence.

The alleged failure of Keynesianism rests on the experience of the recent slump which afflicted all the advanced capitalist states, when recorded unemployment rates rose to the highest levels since the 1930s. But this argument is completely superficial. It precisely ignores the element of deliberate policy choice first in initiating the recession, then in prolonging it once under way, and finally in restraining the process of recovery. Unlike the literal economic breakdown of the Great Depression, the recent slump reflected in large measure a controlled response by the Western states to a situation which was threatening to drift out of control because of the unprecedented acceleration in inflation.

Thus demand management policies can be seen

to have considerably tamed the anarchy of capitalism with respect to the overall level of expenditure
and the level of economic activity. Their very
success in this respect serves to highlight their real
weaknesses and the areas where anarchy still
prevails. One of these is that demand management
operates on a nationally limited scale and hence by
definition leaves untouched those aspects of
anarchy which derive from the relations *between*
states. If, for example, there is a generalised
recession, then any one country which unilaterally
sought to expand would inevitably risk a deterioration in its balance of payments as domestic
growth sucked in imports from abroad without a
matching rise in exports. Going it alone might also
stoke up higher inflationary pressure. This kind of
problem could only be overcome by internationally
co-ordinated economic management. In principle
this is not impossible, but it has proved very
difficult in practice.

A second main residue of anarchy lies in the fact
that although governments can establish a general
climate favourable to private capitalist investment
— via tax incentives, wage restraint, relaxation of
price controls, and the creation of confidence that
if an expansion starts it will not later be cut short
by the need to deal with some pressing weakness —
they cannot by indirect means *force* capitalists to
invest. More precisely, they cannot do so without
either extending the range of controls at their
command or the lengths to which they are prepared
to go in making use of existing controls. Demand
management techniques subject *aggregate* demand

to reasonably predictable influence, but are much less effective in determining the *structure or composition* of demand between private consumption, government spending, exports and private investment.

A third general problem exposed by the relative success of demand management has been that the achievement and maintenance of full employment has deprived capitalism of a vital disciplinary instrument for containing the ability and willingness of the working class to struggle to improve the terms on which its labour power is supplied to employers in both private and public sectors. In Britain this problem has been made worse by the jealously guarded autonomy of the unions and the prevalence of a sectionalised and anarchic system of wages and conditions bargaining. The prolonged suspension of the old disciplinary mechanism of mass unemployment has unleashed new problems of persistent inflation and the assertion of working class priorities within the workplace. The resulting tensions have dramatically highlighted the anarchy of the process of income distribution both between pay as a whole and profits, and amongst different groups of wage and salary earners. Viewed in this light, incomes policies are an attempt to mediate between rival claims on resources, to harmonise the movement of money incomes with some specific definition of national objectives and priorities and to subject the distribution of income to conscious social control. It is this aspect of incomes policies which accounts for the ambivalence of the British Conservative Party towards them.

The fourth, and most pervasive gap within the framework of demand management, is that it requires that *needs* be modified and transformed into *effective demand* through the mediation of money. This is not an insurmountable problem in individual cases. The sick, the old, the disabled and those otherwise disadvantaged can be given pensions and allowances to spend on their individual needs. But broader social needs such as, for example, the improvement of the environment, are less easily made effective. In one sense, the shift of overall economic management away from a reliance on demand towards a reliance on need is the most fundamental problem to be resolved in the building of socialism. It is a problem not for the distant future, but one which is raised at the level of immediate policy, as the debates over nuclear energy or the future of the car industry show.

We have used demand management as one example to demonstrate in some detail how capitalism has responded to strains, in this case caused by the economic anarchy of free market production, by using state intervention to control and minimise such strains. This intervention produces problems of its own to which in turn the state must respond and adapt.

This process is quite general. Advanced capitalism has become socialised to a high degree. Capitalism has only become advanced by accepting its own partial deformation. The strategic task facing socialists is not that of preparing for a seizure of state power in some moment of supreme initiative and then proceeding to construct socialism from scratch. It is rather one of identifying the areas of deformation within capitalism and seeking to push these points of vulnerability as far and as fast as the balance of forces in any given situation will allow. The identification of such points in the specific context of Britain is our next task.

Britain Since The War

Introduction

A theory of social revolution is not born out of logical principles; it is derived from a view of social reality. And because social reality changes, it follows that a theory of revolution must change and not remain fixed in the postures of a previous era.

The idea of revolution presented here represents a break with the classic Leninist tradition in a number of ways. There is little point in trying to stretch one or two ambiguous quotations from Lenin to cover this break.

We will argue that the nature of modern capitalism requires a view of socialist change which lies substantially outside the concept of revolution developed by the Bolshevik Party.

We do not adhere to this position because it is 'pleasant' or 'non-violent' but because it conforms to the reality of modern advanced capitalism. And we do not hold that this reality is less oppressive or violent than that of previous eras; there is no question of revolution being an easier path than before. On the contrary, the fact that oppression is in certain ways even deeper under modern capitalism, means that revolution remains a difficult and dangerous objective.

There can be no question, in this era, of revolution being achieved in some momentary unbalance of capitalist control, by a quick seizure of the levers of power. The most obvious fact of social change is that the enormous and increasing complexity of modern society demands a revolution which is of comparable complexity. Our theory of revolution cannot be simple, and any sloganistic appeal, either to the classic texts of Marx and Lenin on the one hand, or to the power of modern bourgeois democracy on the other, is certain to fail.

The fact of complexity does not mean however that there are not certain strands of economic, social and political development in Britain which can be analysed to give us some grasp of the necessary strategy. This chapter tries to draw out these strands and put them into historical perspective.

Capitalist Restabilisation and Social Crisis

Our starting point is the major paradox of recent history, a paradox whose resolution provides the key to socialist advance. Immediately after the war a series of measures were taken to promote economic stability and prevent a return to the catastrophic economic recession of the '30s. They were undertaken with a recognition that further mass unemployment was socially unacceptable; that the volcano of mass unrest, which had remained quiescent in the pre-war years, would blow up in any post-war depression. Such fears were quite explicit and far from unjustified. Many observers, on both left and right, assumed that an almost automatic recession would occur after a short-lived boom. And most agreed that such a recession would provoke a level of social and political unrest quite different from the '30s. A solid political swing to the left throughout Europe, which had put Communist and Socialist parties to the very edge of power, was interpreted by many to mean that the next stage would be their actual assumption of power during the post-war slump.

In fact the very reverse happened. After a rather shaky start, all the European economies recovered and progressed to a long period of economic success. Growth proceeded at historically unprecedented rates, undisturbed by severe cyclical fluctuations, and low levels of unemployment were in one country after another attained and preserved. This was as true for Britain as for any other country. Comparatively its economic growth was outpaced by most other capitalist countries, but from a historical perspective, the post-war period has been one of boom.

Moreover this economic boom was accompanied by a programme of social reform which changed beyond recognition the day-to-day lives of most of the British people. Many figures can be produced to prove the obvious. To take the most basic parameters of human life: in 1950, infant mortality was 31.4 per 1000 live births; in 1960 it was 22.5; in 1972, 17.6. To take the basic statistics of social existence: in 1961, 22.4% of all households lacked a fixed bath, 6.5% a W.C. and 21.8%, a hot water tap. In 1971 the corresponding percentages were 9.1, 1.1, 6.5 respectively.

Some of these changes, such as the fall in infant mortality, are merely a continuation of long term trends. Others, such as the expansion of mass higher education, are a very pronounced post-war trend. From a secular standpoint one could fix on, say, 1935 as an arbitrary mid-point and move back to 1895 in one direction and 1975 in the other. The first half of this span does, it is true, contain substantial measures of social reform and improvement — compulsory free education to the age of 14, old age pensions, unemployment insurance, council housing, female suffrage, domestic electrification and the wireless. These changes both anticipate those of the second forty years and surpass the standards of the nineteenth century by a margin which stands comparison with the relative advance recorded in the latter period. But this does not alter the major conclusion. For most people, post-war material conditions have improved so radically as to present an almost physical break with the pre-war period. This conclusion should be self-evident. For many Marxists it is not.

The emphasis may seem extreme. Considerable areas of material deprivation continue to exist and it is right that socialists should continually emphasise these and resist the evasion or erosion of standards already achieved. But this endeavour should not obscure the central fact of post war capitalism: that modern capitalist states have overcome their economic contradictions to the point where they can offer the perspective of reasonable *private* prosperity to the *bulk* of their population. Indeed for the majority that is not just a perspective but a reality.

This conclusion is not altered by the current economic recession. We will delay any fuller discussion of this except to point out that on any basis of comparison, whether in actual numbers of unemployed or in the depths of material suffering which the unemployed sustain, the current situation is far less severe than the depressed '30s. Knowledge of this fact should not lead to any complacency about or acquiescence in current unemployment, but it should prevent any unwarranted belief that the good old, bad old days are returning.

Socialists tend to resist this conclusion for historic and agitational reasons. But such resistance obscures the paradox of this situation. Capitalism can offer a perspective of private material prosperity. Yet accompanying this perspective is its twin, a set of social relationships whose poverty and fragmentation matches the increasing levels of private affluence. The last decade has shown that such a society fails to satisfy large sections of its members *whatever* their level of private prosperity.

The socialist movement has been haunted by the fear that if it were to be proved wrong about the necessity of the economic collapse of capitalism, then socialism could be indefinitely held off by a process of crude material corruption. This fear, which was sometimes expressed as a puritanical disapproval of·material benefit, has been abruptly rebutted. The age of colour TV and package holidays has also proved to be an age of social upheaval and discontent, deeper and more pervasive than anything seen in Britain for 60 or 70 years.

This discontent moreover stems from and, in its articulate forms, is directed against, gaps and flaws in social relationships and social control which, unlike material want, are extremely difficult to remedy under capitalism. Indeed much contemporary insecurity and discontent arises directly from the forms which economic prosperity has taken. In order to satisfy the material aspirations it arouses, capitalist mass production of mass consumption relies on processes of wage bargaining which destabilise economic and social equilibrium by contributing to persistent and chronic inflation.

Similarly, as we noted in above, the pattern of values produced and demanded under post-war capitalist affluence, nurtures a way of life which bypasses and even detracts from the satisfaction of such social needs as environmental protection, resource conservation, community integration or the socialisation of child care. Socialism has re-emerged as a necessity not as in the past to rectify gross deficiencies in economic mechanisms, but as a solution to these new social crises.

There is an odd irony in this situation, that the working out of such a precise dialectic should produce such confusion amongst the guardians of dialectics. Capitalism has checked and in many ways subdued its inherent economic anarchy and restrained the economic collapse which Marxism saw as its inevitable end. But by limiting the economic contradiction, a whole series of social and ideological contradictions have been triggered, which are much more difficult for capitalism to control. Yet a substantial part of the left, in particular those who are organised Marxists, have been so obsessed by economic contradiction that they have tried to squeeze such social discontent back into the economic box. The issue of workers' control of production, for example, has emerged almost spontaneously as a major component of workplace struggles. However, the attention paid by the left to this issue, in the way of pressing for immediate changes in the area of control, has been minimal in comparison with the attention paid to the wages struggle. The same comparison could be made in many other spheres.

The difficulty is partly one of history, that Marxists have only just begun to forge the tools to enable them to understand historical development in other than purely economic terms. And this is a great defect in analysing the history of the last 25 years in Britain.

There is a tempting historical parrallel between the '70s and the first decade of this century. Seventy years ago, Britain was emerging from the first of its periods of great economic expansion. Internationally, more modern industrial powers were nibbling at British markets and threatening its imperial hegemony. At home society was wracked with dispute; widespread and bitter industrial action was being taken against cuts in real wages; unions were challenging attempts to restrict their powers; women were threatening violent struggle to win the vote; nationalist conflict erupted in Ireland. There was a pervasive feeling that an era was ending and that new social forces were emerging.

In the end, the parallel cannot be pushed too far. Yet there is a real sense in which there is a continuity between 1912 and 1978, as though for the intervening years Britain had been kept on ice with social forces maturing but never reaching any point of qualitative change. There has been after all no substantial change in the structure and balance of British politics since 1924, when Labour finally replaced Liberal as the major working class vote-winner, and that was no more than a seal upon a process essentially completed by 1912. Nor did the labour movement emerge from the institutional and ideological isolation imposed in 1926 until the last decade. Overall this kind of frozen historical continuity is the most obvious characteristic of British society; everything changes but all remains the same. The dominant feature of the *current* situation is that the crisis of social relations has been transposed to a higher level by the degree of economic progress.

This process, whereby social contradictions have tended to overlay economic contradictions as the major source of political change, is not confined to Britain; it has to some degree touched all advanced capitalist countries. What has characterised Britain in the post war period is that *relative* decline and failure in an international context have been superimposed on a historically successful period of economic growth. It is the combination of this relative decline with the very advanced social integration of Britain that has produced chronic social unease.

The Legacy of Empire

The relative decline of Britain as an imperial power has been proceeding for many years. In economic terms the crossover from dominance to decline can be placed as early as 1870 at the transition from an iron-based to a steel-based economy. Politically the dating is later, perhaps into the early years of the twentieth century. But leaving precise timescales aside, Britain has for many years suffered from the effects of a decline in international status. From being the major world power it has become one of the poorer and least powerful of a dozen advanced capitalist countries. However it is only the post-war period that the full consequences of imperial decay have become evident.

In the years immediately after the war, the advantages which British capitalism had derived from the Empire were removed by the USA as a price to be paid for wartime loans. Henceforth Britain was left with only the distortions and negative effects. The economic handicaps are in some ways the easiest to analyse, though in the last instance they are not the most important.

These include first, an orientation towards military expenditure which went beyond the high (though declining) proportion of national income devoted to arms. What proved to be equally important was the persistent tendency of State intervention in production and investment to be concentrated on those sectors with some special relevance to national security.

Second, the financial sectors of British capital were dominated by overseas interests rather than the supply of finance to home-based British industry. This did not lead directly to any under-financing of British industry, though it is possible that the type of finance normally made available (based on short-term overdrafts rather than long-term loans), inhibited growth in new and technically advanced industries. What is more important is that the influence of city financial interests tended to distort government policy on exchange rates and capital control, even though the actual economic benefits of City banking were financially small and the political importance of the international financial sector was becoming irrelevant.

Third, British industry had to make a much greater accommodation to post-war economic trends than other advanced capitalist countries. British trade was based on selling low grade goods to underdeveloped countries in return for food and raw materials. It is an interesting myth that Britain was ever renowned for high quality and technically advanced manufacturers. The post-war resurgence of world trade was heavily biased towards trade between advanced countries in manufactured goods, a trend to which European history was historically better adapted. Britain's technical backwardness was continually emphasised as modern manufacturing techniques were used to produce high grade consumer goods as well as capital equipment.

A final economic distortion was the low domestic investment ratio (that is the proportion of national income devoted to fixed investment) brought about by the historic tendency of British industry to invest abroad. The period when this was most important was at the end of the nineteenth century, when up to 9% of British national income was invested overseas. This was over half of the total of all investment and was accompanied by a fall in domestic investment rather than a cut in consumption.

This economic strategy had been quite rational from a capitalist standpoint and it undoubtedly extended the period of British international dominance long after this was justified on the basis of home industrial performance. It also played an important part in sustaining the home economy from 1890 to 1914 when substantial trade deficits in goods and services were more than compensated by the inflow of interest and dividends. The freedom this gave to maintain cheap food supplies, for example, undoubtedly strengthened the hand of capital in a time of mounting social discontent.

The repercussions of this era, when international economic strength counterbalanced low domestic growth, impinged on the post-war period in two ways. First, the level of investment was low by comparison with most of Britain's competitors. Second there was some tendency for capital to be invested overseas rather than at home, though the quantitative significance of overseas investment should not be overstated; it rarely exceeded 1 or

2% of national income, a fifth of the proportion sustained in the heyday of Empire. More important than the crude relative volumes of private overseas and domestic investment, was the fact that British big capital maintained its characteristic pattern of defensive domestic investment which complemented existing products and processes, and tended to locate its innovative ventures overseas, thus perpetuating the home economy's technical backwardness.

The economic legacy of imperialism is, however, insufficient in itself to explain the post-war problems of the British economy. In fact, by the early '60s, this inheritance was of diminished rather than enhanced importance. The physical withdrawal from Empire had undercut the major rationale for high arms expenditures and this was reflected in a lower proportionate allocation of resources. Moreover it had been recognised that a more even handed and planned intervention in industry by the state was required. Private capital outflow was balanced by increasing overseas investment in Britain, often in those areas of new technology which domestic industry had neglected. The investment ratio had shown consistent increases since the early '50s, and British industry had undertaken a considerable switch into export markets to compensate for the loss of income caused by the sale of portfolio investment during the Second World War.

The crucial question is not how an imperial legacy pulled Britain behind in the '50s, but why it was, that when the effects of this legacy had largely worn off, the British economy actually declined still further relative to other advanced countries. Two other factors must be considered before this can be tackled: the role of the state and the position of the British working class. These two related factors define the specific features of the post-war period as distinct from those discussed above which define its historical continuity.

The Role of the State

It is a cliché that the post-war resurgence of capitalism was based on state intervention, and yet it is difficult to enlarge this statement except by detailed comparative analysis. There are very few state functions which cannot be considered as long term trends with little or no differentiation between the pre-and post-war periods. There is also very little uniformity of state intervention across advanced capitalist countries and it is arguable that the two most dynamic economies – Germany and Japan – have shown the least overt state activity.

The most general characterisation of what is distinctive about post-war state intervention lies in the conscious recognition of the need for social regulation and control over the functioning of the economy, rather than the use of state intervention to cover ad hoc needs. Whether undertaken to promote long term objectives or in response to short term crises, state intervention has super-imposed certain long term patterns on economic and social life. Such intervention has been described in terms of planning, though a full appreciation of its extent and depth requires wider horizons, which take into account both international control and regulation, and also the incorporation of certain social aspirations, such as low unemployment and social welfare benefits, into a general consensus of accepted standards. The examples of Germany and Japan show that certain of the most specific forms of intervention such as actual economic planning and investment control need not function within precisely defined state agencies. In both these countries, and in particular, Japan, planning was carried out behind a screen of market competition which disguised the reality of a high degree of financial integration and control.

What was common was the *conscious* recognition of the need for control, that is the superseding of certain aspects of market anarchy by some kind of centralised direction. This was not entirely unforeseen by Marxists; some important work had been done in the early part of the century on the development of a state monopoly capitalism with a number of these features. What was not foreseen was, first, the comparatively benign nature of this new system in which a considerable share of growing prosperity was passed on to the working class. The contrast with, say, Bukharin's vision of a terrifying slave machine dragging down the vast majority into pitiless degradation, is very marked. Undoubtedly, the reason for this divergence is an underestimation of the power of bourgeois democracy to deliver welfare benefits and act as a buffer in social conflict.

The second unforeseen factor was the drawing

together of capitalist nation states, under the general domination of USA, to provide mechanisms for the containment of international rivalries. The Bretton Woods Agreement, the EEC, NATO, GATT, OECD, IMF, BIS, and so on through the alphabet, provided robust ways of negotiating differences, ways which have in fact shown their underlying power in the wake of the breakdown of many *formal* international financial arrangements after 1971. The world capitalist system has experienced in succession the American withdrawal from a gold standard; floating exchange rates; the oil crisis and the avalanche of 'petrodollars'; major bank collapses in Germany, America, Italy and Britain; world recession and the collapse of speculative booms in oil tankers and property. Its stability in the face of these shocks has been remarkable. There has been a notable absence of 'beggar-my-neighbour' exchange rate manipulation, trade and tariff wars, or debt foreclosures, all of which were confidently predicted.

It is of course an open question how long this willingness to accept international negotiation will continue under the strain of such buffeting; but its strength over the past 25 years has been growing rather than declining.

In both these areas, the key element has been that the state has elevated long term social and economic stability above the short term interests of capitalist firms.

State intervention has two general purposes: to stabilise the functioning of the economic and social system within tolerable bounds, and to promote the release of productive forces to achieve higher growth. These may not always be in harmony and they are certainly not present in equal measure in all capitalist states. The specifically *British* aspect of state intervention is the heavy emphasis on stabilisation and the comparative failure of such productive intervention as has been undertaken.

In the economic sphere, this emphasis meant that Keynesian demand management was a major concern rather than investment planning or control. In the social sphere it meant an increasing volume of welfare payments and services, housing, health and education, which became the main components of government expenditure. The total volume of such expenditure was only marginally greater than in most other advanced capitalist countries; what was particularly evident in Britain was the constant elaboration of a central state bureaucratic system which became increasingly autonomous both in its modes of operation and in its freedom from accountability. Thus while some kind of state-controlled health service has been a feature of most capitalist countries, only in Britain has it become divorced from individual insurance contributions and become a service financed out of general taxation and administered by a central government authority.

State intervention is, as we have noted, the characterising feature of post-war capitalism. State activity has been directed towards the defence and development of capitalist society, tasks in which it has achieved a large measure of success. But the basic connection of state activity with capitalism should not obscure the fact that such intervention is invariably contradictory. It always contains elements which are antagonistic to the operation of capitalism. It undermines private ownership or distorts the operations of the market or socialises certain issues previously considered as purely individual. Whatever the precise nature of this deformation process, it is this component of state intervention which can have very important though unintended consequences.

The social and political consequences of state intervention have been taken to a higher pitch in Britain than in other capitalist countries, to the point where state intervention constitutes one of the major contradictions of British society. A large state sector has evolved, unconstrained by the normal disciplines and objectives of private enterprise, but at the same time not democratically linked to the requirements of the mass of the people as it would be under a socialist system. It is this advanced socialising effect of British state intervention which has emerged as a major point of current social and political conflict.

We should note that this analysis of the state does not, in any sense, remove the state into a position of class neutrality. The state apparatus, defined rather specifically as the Administrative grades of the Civil Service, army officers, senior policemen and sections of local government administrators, are undoubtedly committed to the preservation of capitalism. Moreover the *general* purpose of the state, defined much more broadly as the overall intent, structure and hierarchy of all state institutions, is usually concerned at least to preserve the status quo. What we have emphasised is that state activity, concerned to plan and co-ordinate capitalism must lead to acute contradictions. These form a focus and arena for struggle. This is heightened by the alleged class neutrality of the state which is required, at least in its normal functioning, to preserve the appearance of 'fairness' and 'even-handedness'.

The fact that in moments of crisis, the state apparatus will tend to throw its weight behind the preservation of capitalism is a crucial matter in deciding how socialists should act in such crises. But this does not reduce state action in normal times to a mere facade, a propaganda cloak for the real purposes of the state.

In addition the growing employment in the state sector means that an ever larger number of people are removed from the immediate strictures of private capitalism. The fact that these people may, in some indirect way, be working with the overall intent of preserving capitalism does not prevent them from developing a perception of their position which is at variance with this.

The Strength of the Working Class

The second important specific feature of post-war Britain has been the exceptionally powerful position of the working class. There are two sources of this power. The main source is a simple consequence of the advanced social character of British capitalism. The working class is, and has been for several generations, numerically dominant. No significant

peasant class has existed in Britain for 150 years
and even agricultural wage labourers have been
reduced to the smallest proportion of any major
capitalist country. The independent and semi-
independent petit-bourgeois and professional classes
have largely been squeezed into various kinds of
dependent relations with either the state or large
companies. Independent capitalists have been
reduced by many years of merger, takeover and
bankruptcy to a relatively small role.

In these circumstances, the working class has
emerged not only as the dominant numerical class
but increasingly as the dominant social force. The
consequences of this are of the utmost political
importance.

It is true that this massive expansion of the
working class has meant that the social functioning
of this class has become very varied and diverse.
Marxist class theory has scarcely begun to appreciate this and has, as yet, produced few tools of
analysis other than mere observations. However
the attempt to deny the expansion, to define the
working class as being no more than the traditional
male, manual, manufacturing employee of the
Industrial Revolution seems a curious and perverse
attempt to crush reality into a prefabricated
theoretical box. Simple observation may be a poor
theoretical tool, but the dogmatic application of
poor theory is worse.

This numerical and social strength would be
much less important but for the second source of
power: the strength and continuity of working
class organisation. The British trade union move-

ment has been developed for a hundred years; it has organised the main areas of the industrial working class for over sixty years. The normal processes of electoral democracy have functioned for a hundred years with a considerable degree of mass suffrage and for fifty years with both universal suffrage and a dominant working class party capable of challenging for government.

The situation is almost unparalleled. Almost all continential European labour movements (the exceptions are in Scandinavia) have been literally destroyed at least once, whilst the processes of electoral democracy have been similarly disrupted. The American labour movement has encompassed mass unionisation only since the late '30s in any effective sense, whist the peculiar ethnic and cultural gulfs within the American working class have long retarded the growth of a truly working class party.

The only significant European movements which run counter to this generalisation point up a subsidiary factor which gives the British working class enhanced strength. This is that despite its power and organisation, the British trade union movement has, until recently , been relatively unincorporated in the British political structure.

This is not inconsistent with the dominance of a reformist ideology within the trade union movement. The unions have remained true to the original conception of their role as bodies representing working class interests, but within an accepted capitalist political framework. British trade union leaders have, with a handful of exceptions, played a passive political role, acting only in a negative fashion to support the generally right wing leaders of the Labour Party. This retention of autonomy has often been regarded as reactionary, and indeed it was so when union block votes were cast with no more intention than to sustain the Labour Party's right wing. But its final product has been a union rank and file led by shop stewards with an independence and combativeness un-matched in any capitalist country. This indepen-dence has been inevitably eroded in recent years, particularly as Labour governments have become more normal, but it is still a powerful force. The Scandinavian unions, under the influence of continuous Social Democratic governments do not possess this degree of autonomy.

Working class power has a number of con-sequences. Not all are confined to Britain but all have been more prominent in Britain than else-where. One of the most general is a simple feature of bourgeois democracy, and is one of the main sources of political contradiction in modern capitalist society. It is that a political body which, in theory, holds supreme power will always tend to appease the numerical majority of those who elect it, if only because of individual political ambitions.

This countervailing trend within the political functioning of the state is often ignored by Marxist theorists as being too subjective or encouraging reformist illusions, but it nevertheless remains as an effective force. Its result is that the role of the state as a defender of capitalism becomes muffled and riddled by internal contradictions.

A number of other consequences follow from the power of the British working class.

First, in the absence of a significant reserve of unemployed labour, workers have the ability to exert a continuous pressure on money wage levels which, in the context of an increasingly monopolised industry with less price competition, has contributed to the emergence of inflation as the main economic problem of advanced capitalism.

Second, they are able to inhibit the introduction of new techniques and methods of production where these offer no short term benefits, or to extract a high price for co-operation in terms of new pay scales, and manning agreements.

Third, they can obtain increasingly high levels of government welfare expenditure both on transfer payments such as unemployment benefit or pensions or on real resource expenditure on health, housing and education.

This third point must be distinguished from the first two in that working class pressure on government expenditure does not act directly at the point of production but via a rather subtle series of pressures centred around Parliament and local councils. The finally determining factor has been the use of bourgeois democracy, but specific events have usually been more decisively influenced by the characteristically British networks of committees and pressure groups which have pushed through most of the social advances of the last thirty years. One of the most interesting features of this period has been the persistent tendency of committees of 'eminent' people from Beveridge to Bullock to urge measures favourable to the working class in the name of minimising social conflict.

It is of course one of the major contradictions of bourgeois democracy, and one to which we will return, that although it offers considerable power to affect the disposition of resources, it allows no effective control over their day-to-day management. Health services or education or social welfare may be greatly expanded, but their control rests firmly in the hands of a professional or bureaucratic elite.

It can be objected that the end result of these three lines of influence has not always been of unqualified benefit. Pressure on money wages has been neutralised by endemic inflation. Power to resist technological change has often resulted in low productivity and, eventually, redundancy. Government expenditure has been largely financed by increased working class taxation rather than any substantial redistribution of income and wealth. This illustrates the contradictions of working class power as it is at present exerted. that it is concerned with short term gain and not long term control; it is negative rather than positive. But to invoke this contradiction, to deny the reality of even short term power, is to deny the major political perspective of our time.

The justification for this assertion lies in answering the question posed above: why Britain, have proceeded so far down the road to post-imperial adjustment, failed to take the final steps.

The 1960s: Modernisation Stalled

The analysis so far is one of a society hampered by the legacy of Empire and with a strong and combative working class capable of resisting any attempts at change which threatened jobs or living standards. It portrays a country being strangled by its own history. Left in this state the analysis is incomplete and misleading.

The post-war history of the advanced capitalist countries exhibits various approaches to the problems posed by the need on the one hand to modernise and transform industry in order to achieve a high level of technological development, and on the other to satisfy the social requirements of the working class. Different countries faced these problems in different mixes and produced different solutions. Only a handful of countries developed in a relatively smooth fashion, notably the defeated powers, Germany and Japan. In these states, defeat enabled demands to be placed on the working class, which might otherwise have been resisted. The depression of living standards and assertion of capitalist control in the labour process cleared the way for high rates of investment and technical innovation. In other countries various political, social and economic barriers had to be overcome. In France there was the Gaullist reformation of political institutions; in America the insistence by the Kennedy and Johnson administrations in the early 1960s on the application of Keynesian management methods; in Italy the use of state holding companies as the levers of economic progress. Each of these methods of reform enabled a period of stagnation to be overcome.

Britain had, as we have described, severe impediments in the way of any equivalent modernising process derived from its imperial past. It would be a mistake however to underestimate the degree to which these barriers were, if not entirely removed, at least lowered in the '50s.

The actual political process of withdrawing from Empire was carried through reasonably smoothly with a degree of resilience and freedom from bitterness notably lacking in the comparable French experience. Moreover in the sphere of trade, British industry made reasonably successful efforts to increase its exports of manufactured goods and, in particular, to adjust to new markets and new products. There was a steady decrease in the burden of overseas military expenditure, and of arms expenditure in general, in proportion to the national income. And, in a very general sense, the British labour movement was brought to the brink of a systematic co-operation with capitalism. The most obvious symbol of this was the negotiations with the miners, hitherto the most strike-prone section of British labour, who in the early 1960s agreed to a massive rundown of pits and consequent loss of jobs.

The period from roughly 1962 to 1968 constitutes the most crucial phase of post-war development, for it was then that the attempt was made to take Britain through its own process of modernisation. It was, of course, an unequivocal failure. But this was by no means an obvious outcome, for the effort represented the most sustained and conscious undertaking by any capitalist country.

In external relations, the decision to enter the EEC was taken with a very wide degree of political agreement. Internally a whole range of new government measures were adopted to promote the planning and development of industry.

The Conservative 'Neddies' were taken over and enlarged by Labour to culminate in the National Plan of 1965, whilst efforts were made in cotton, coal and shipbuilding to rationalise these once dominant but now decaying sectors. At a more general level, there was a concentrated effort to understand the methods whereby continental Europe had managed to emerge as so much more economically dynamic than Britain and, in particular, how state intervention could succeed in those areas of production hitherto ignored. The experience of the French in indicative planning was particularly influential. The Robbins Report was universally accepted as pointing to crucial weaknesses in the system of training engineers and scientists and a major and rapid expansion of higher education was initiated.

In industrial relations, the Donovan Commission was notable for its sober acceptance of the rights of trade unions and the need to control maverick employers as well as militant trade unionists. There was an incipient move to place wage bargaining on a new footing, with productivity replacing crude power struggles as the determining factor. The classic Fawley agreement was widely regarded as a model for the future.

The detailed functioning of the State machine was closely scrutinised. The Fulton committee reported on the need to introduce a much wider and more integrated range of skills into the central Civil Service. A number of new and, in intention, innovatory ministries were created — Economic Affairs, Technology, Land and Natural Resources. New state agencies such as the Industrial Re-organisation Corporation were set up to provide a means of encouraging mergers, rationalising manufacture and providing risk capital.

There was also a widespread acceptance amongst leading industrialists and commentators that the Labour Party was the appropriate political vehicle for conducting this modernisation process. This was of course an attempt to bring the Labour Party and, indirectly, the trade unions in from the cold, so as not to repeat the vicious antagonisms of the Attlee era. It did however imply a recognition that political and social concessions would be made as the price for incorporation.

It is easy now to caricature the era of "white hot technology"; what is overlooked is that it was the one period in post-war British history when a progressive, modernising government came even close to forming any kind of national consensus of support. The reasons for its failure are crucial to understanding the current impasse of British capitalism.

The only developed account of the failure of the Labour government of this period, apart from propagandistic claims that it practised either too much or too little socialism, emphasises its purely technical failures with respect to devaluation and the control of capital. Success, it is argued, lay within reach if only devaluation had not been delayed, or if only tight regulations had been imposed on the legendary Zurich gnomes. There may be some truth in this, but it hardly answers the point. If the blame is laid on bad technical advice then it must be asked either why no good advice was forthcoming, or why it was rejected. Why, for example, did the British government hesitate to use measures which had been used with considerable success by the Gaullist government a few years previously?

The problem has to be transposed to a different level from that of technical economic controls. It can only be handled within the broadest kind of social and cultural perspective. In the final analysis, the efforts to modernise British industry in the mid-60s failed not because of economic backwardness, but because of the very advanced nature of Britain's social relations. Modernisation requires a class, or at least a class sector, which is clearly identified with, and benefits from the process. Moreover it requires that class to have some power of moral and ideological dominance. It requires, in short, a class dynamic. Britain, then, as now, possessed no such class grouping. To the contrary, it possessed an organised working class which, in certain key areas such as engineering, was if anything opposed to modernisation, and which was resistant to the calls for national or class unity.

This period saw the fruition of the shop steward movement, built up over many years of detailed plant level bargaining, and unique to Britain. This movement combined a deep hostility to factory-level innovations, which normally manifested themselves in the short term as manning reductions and the removal of bargaining power away from the stewards and into the official union structure, with the lack of a wider perspective for strategic political change. This strong corporate outlook, later to prove a double edged weapon, effectively prevented the shop stewards from being incorporated into the process of modernisation and enabled them to resist, though not without some hard struggles, the productivity deals which were a key feature of the moves towards industrial revitalisation.

Not that industrial capitalists needed much pressure to put off new development. The sloth and inefficiency of British management was already legendary and most of British industry responded to the prodding of the Industrial Reorganisation Corporation or MinTech with little more than a shrug and a ready acceptance of any subsidies going. And the higher reaches of the Civil Service, when asked to emulate the feats of the French 'polytechniciens', responded by burying all innovation under a web of committees.

This lack of dynamism is not simply attributable to monopoly control in industry though that has played its part. Rather it is the social consequence of imperialism, which produced a ruling class culturally removed from production and an intelligentsia committed to ideas of public service combined with a safe income from government stocks. It is often said that, the British ruling class is the cleverest in the world and to a degree this is true. Certainly in developing a bourgeois hegemony which welded together a harmonious social system it has been very successful. It is however the very success of this bourgeois synthesis which has enabled the class structure of Britain to develop so smoothly, has enabled the structure of bourgeois democracy to develop such autonomous importance, and has enabled the British working class to gain such concrete power.

The final death blow to the possibility that a modernising Labour government might alter the economic dynamic of Britain came not from a narrow economic issue or indeed from any struggle based purely at the point of production. Rather it came from the social upheavals of the late '60s.

Social Control and the Subversion of Bourgeois Hegemony

The exact cause of the great international explosion of 1968 is not clear; though it was a social and political phenomenon without parallel, transcending even the Year of Revolution, 1848, in its international scope. There was certainly an element of international emulation heightened by the use, almost for the first time, of virtually instantaneous satellite TV transmissions. The images of that year still stand to mind; the NLF flags on Hue Citadel; clenched fists of black athletes in Mexico City; the CRS visors and shields appearing out of teargas clouds in Paris; bewildered Russian tank crews harassed by Prague crowds; the ruins of Detroit ghettos. Yet each of these events and the accompanying discord of a hundred cities (even London, where a Vietnam march in November 1968 was seriously seen in the leader column of the *Times* as being the precursor to armed uprising) was its own endpoint, the result of apparently dissimilar movements within quite different societies.

We do not propose to analyse this international shock wave except to note one factor. All the popular movements we have mentioned were failures, at least in the dimension of physical repression. Even the Tet Offensive was accounted a material defeat at the time. But each, with one exception, set in motion powerful forces for change which, in some cases, are still progressing. The Tet Offensive broke the power of the US government to convince its own people that the price was worth the gain and initiated a deep questioning of the effectiveness of political democracy in controlling the actions of governments. In Italy and France, the Communist Parties began their climb out of the political wilderness. In the USA, the struggle against racism was given a political dimension which it had never achieved before. What they all represented (save the Tet which lies outside this circle except in its indirect effects on the American people) was a break with certain aspects of bourgeois hegemony rather than a challenge to state power. And what they demonstrated more effectively than a thousand theories was that such challenges could emerge out of popular movements; that they need not be mediated by any strata of intellectuals or party groups; that bourgeois hegemony within the political and ideological structures of society is not absolute.

The one exception was of course Prague, which demonstrated the appalling truth that the Eastern European countries can, for the moment, be repressed and controlled by simple coercion in a way which is impossible in advanced capitalist states.

The British experience at the end of the '60s was in some ways milder than elsewhere but it was no less decisive. It contained a number of strands. First there was the extension of struggle at the point of production beyond the normal processes of wage bargaining and into areas which directly challenged the rights of private ownership. The causes of this are not clear (this is true of much of this explosion of social movements), though it may be connected to the international pressure on British industry working its way through historically declining industries like coal and textiles into previously expanding areas of engineering. It was only in the '60s that these felt significant import pressures in the British market. Be that as it may (and the connection is rather loose) there developed an increasing tendency for workers to intervene in closures or changes in production patterns. This tendency reached a historic focus in the UCS work-in which marked a decisive change in industrial relations, setting in motion the process which culminated in the recent Bullock Report.

Second, social movements developed at the community level around issues previously removed from conscious political struggle. The environmental movement is largely fueled by this sense of community preservation, whilst the squatting movement forms its most obvious backbone. The squatters revealed in another sphere a phenomenon that we have already mentioned, the challenging of private property rights, this time over housing rather than productive facilities.

Third, areas of human life previously considered private and non-political were brought into the arena of political struggle. The most important of these is the women's movement, though what is encompassed within this general area is in fact a much larger shift in the manner in which people perceive the relation between their personal life and society at large.

Fourth, there was a substantial upsurge of social and political consciousness amongst various professional sections of society; doctors, lawyers, scientists and so on. The most fundamental of these occurred in education where a very large change occurred in a very short time in the attitude of teachers towards the nature and purpose of their jobs. This change has gone far enough to be considered as almost the established wisdom, though the recent campaigns aimed at the return of results — orientated education shows how precarious the gains have been. In various other professions the changes have been less obvious and confined to smaller groups. But these have asserted with growing confidence a doctrine of social responsibility in their professional tasks.

Fifth, there has been a steady growth in the

importance of nationalism in Scotland, Wales and in Northern Ireland, though the course of events in this last region owes more to long term historical factors.

These movements display a bewildering variety but they share a common feature. They are not immediately political in the narrow sense that they consciously aim to change the state. (The obvious exception is nationalism. This stands outside the other movements, though even here Welsh nationalism has until now been largely a cultural movement which has chosen the bourgeois democratic process to express itself.) This fact has led socialist political groups to treat them with some scorn though their success in actually achieving social change has been far greater than that of any overtly political group.

They are all concerned with issues which are striking both in their directions and in their subversive force. They challenge some of the most important supports of capitalist society. In essence they are all socialising movements. The tendency of their demands and actions is towards the surpassing of private and individual rights and their replacement with collective responsibilities and rights. This is the common factor which links resistance to the exercise of property rights in closing factories or keeping houses empty or the rights of private sexual oppression, or the ideology of exclusive professional responsibility and control.

This common factor also provides a clue to the reasons for the emergence of these social movements. It is no accident that they have coincided with the development of advanced capitalism. For not only are they unique, but it is inconceivable that they could have asserted themselves at any earlier historical stage. Women, for example, have expressed their rights to sexual liberation before. What they have not done hitherto is to assert these as collective rights requiring structural social reform rather than as expressions of individual freedom.

The importance of these new social movements lies in this coincidence with the patterns of advanced capitalism. They emerge not directly out of the straightforward oppressions and exploitations of capitalism, though it is these they challenge, but rather out of the processes used by capitalism to legitimate and reproduce itself. They are in a sense the products of the the contradictions of bourgeois hegemony for, as we have noted, the major task of post-war capitalism has been for the *state* to modify and socialise various anarchic freedoms of the market and to take over the running of large areas of the economy. This legitimation and stabilisation of capitalism has produced striking results in terms of social stability and economic growth. Its end product is to open up wider and wider areas of society for collective responsibility, even if the intention has been to confine responsibility and control to an ordered and restrained state machine. But if the state ultimately fails to deliver the goods then the next step, towards social responsibility *outside* the confines of the state machine, is easy to take — at least by comparison with a period when the alternatives were pure private ownership or socialism.

In simple terms, if a worker is confronted with a factory closure under a pure private enterprise system, it is a much smaller jump to occupy that factory if a stream of state subsidy and control has previously nurtured it, and if other factories had already been taken over by the state under similar circumstances. Or if the state accepts a major responsibility for providing housing, and regards homelessness, at least *in theory,* as a social rather than a private problem, it becomes a much easier step to take over a vacant house whether council or private. It is after all only carrying out a function that the state has, again in theory, accepted that it *ought* to perform. This does not mean that the extension of these actions to a wider sphere, outside an immediate personal involvement, is straightforward, but it is an important first step.

Conclusion

We have described Britain since the war as a country limited in economic growth and falling behind international competitors to produce a situation of chronic economic weakness. Yet it is simultaneously an advanced capitalist country. In terms of its social relations it is probably the most advanced of all states. The size, maturity and power of its working class combined with the socialising effects of state activity have pushed it to the frontiers of capitalist social development at the same time as retarding its economic progress. The consequence is a society very heavily strained by social conflict and with a ruling class too weak, or perhaps too decadent, to produce a base of its own with sufficient dynamism to modernise its economic structures. However the social conflict has not developed a conscious political purpose; there is no mass socialist movement to work towards the transformation of the state. Instead diverse groups work at subverting capitalism when the need is to build socialism. The fact that the difference between these tasks is not understood on the left is a measure of the problem. This conclusion emphasises that up to now consciously socialist groups have achieved peripheral political effect. They have tended to follow rather than lead social changes. It also emphasises the fragile nature of the balance of forces which exists at the present time. Capitalism inherently reacts to overcome crises; that is its main strength. There is undoubtedly a danger that the advanced nature of social forces in Britain will be perverted into a new type of social corporatism to sustain capitalism. This would be the ultimate 'passive revolution'. There is also the possibility of achieving socialism.

The Policies of Hegemony

Introduction

We have discussed the theoretical base for a political programme centred around the concept that revolutionary change will be achieved not by any single decisive act, but by a continuous development of working class hegemony. It remains to outline the policies associated with such a programme and the political structures necessary to implement it. We will look at the former in this chapter and at the latter in the next.

There is, it must be admitted, a problem about proposing policy. In contrast to the politics of the revolutionary moment, the essence of any hegemonic position is the specificity of its policies, the actual practical propositions which it puts forward. Without this understanding discussions about hegemonic policies tends to drift into vague humanistic generalisations about democracy and the development of human potential hardly distinguishable from the most mundane reformism. The fact that the striking of intransigent and doctrinaire attitudes of revolutionary fervour often conceals conservative and stagnant policy in real situations, should not obscure the equal truth that passive reformism is an ever present danger in the formulation of what we are calling the policies of hegemony. Only in the context of a specific issue can this danger be avoided.

Nor does it help that the processes whereby hegemony is formed are often reduced to a superficial and one-dimensional concentration on propaganda rather than the working out of real interventions in the processes of society. It must be continually re-emphasised that bourgeois hegemony is not a purely intellectual construction produced by clever use of the media or manipulation of political institutions; it operates at a much deeper and more complex level of human society. The consequence of this is that bourgeois hegemony cannot be challenged just by propaganda or by a more-or-less sophisticated form of political exposé. It has to be broken by actual intervention in specific areas to bring about changes, which can be appreciated and assimilated into people's lives, into their everyday experience.

The great power of bourgeois domination lies not so much in its power of repression as in its ability to adapt, to incoporate new ideas and movements, to remain perpetually in a state of change. This more than anything else is the problem to be solved by socialists; to be themselves more adaptable, more able to pay regard to popular forces, more alert for areas of weakness in the enemy than the well-developed agencies of bourgeois control.

An example of this process is the environmental movement. Over the past few years, this movement, particularly in the USA, has put forward demands which are enormously subversive to the future of capitalism. This fact is not welcomed by many 'revolutionaries' who disapprove of the class background or the stated political horizons of many environmentalists. It is true, nevertheless, that a challenge to the rights of private (or for that matter public) industry to ravage the natural environment with little or no control is often a much more fundamental issue than a strike for higher wages. However, involved in any environmental campaign are a set of choices and perspectives which are often perceived as contradictory to other progressive aims; the most obvious is the crude choice between jobs or pollution control. The manner in which the state seeks to use these contradictions in order to restrict environmental control, but also simultaneously seeks to absorb the aura of environmental goodness to maintain its own dominance, is an object lesson in how bourgeois hegemony is maintained. The exercise is not just one of propaganda. In the USA, very important gains have been made in applying environmental controls on industry. Yet at the same time strenuous efforts are made to keep the changes within the bounds of US capitalist freedoms. For example, essentially technical controls are introduced rather than any structural changes in the industrial economy. Huge sums are spent on buying control equipment from private industry, which are then recouped by higher prices, instead of any attempt being made to control by conservation or the use of alternative technologies.

In this context, socialists have to wage a very skilful struggle, rejecting crude choices which imply that jobs or the supply of material goods must be linked with environmental destruction, but also recognising that real choices do have to be made and priorities set. Concessions offered by the state have to be exposed for their inadequacy, but they have to be used to their fullest extent to form a developed base for future demands. And in the course of such struggle, which forms just one restricted area of social and political engagement, the right links have to be made and account taken of comparable struggles being waged by other groups in other areas.

The difficulty of this task, which has to be performed throughout society, is not greatly lessened by propounding generalities, but there are certain basic themes which run through most areas of policy and which act to draw them together.

1. From Economic Corporatism to Hegemonic Bloc

The first is the struggle to transcend the economic corporatism of particular social groups and to promote a deeper and wider social unity. It is a commonplace on the left that a major instrument of social control is the fragmentation of the working class into separate groupings conscious only of their sectional interests and prepared to defend these at the expense of other working class groups. This sense of economic corporatism, is, in itself, an advance on the pure individualism which can be regarded as the most basic reflection of capitalist social relations. In the shape, say, of craft unionism it has in its time been progressive. However, this economic corporatism can assume a decidedly ambiguous role in the current situation. Its maintenance acts as a major stumbling block to any attempt to modernise and regenerate capitalism, but it can also act to retard the development of the wider social perspective necessary for socialist advance.

The problem of sectionalism cannot be resolved by abstract slogans. Simple appeals to some ideal of national unity or to some alleged objective, common interest in opposition to monopoly capitalism will not do. We have emphasised that socialist forces must allow themselves to be limited to purely propagandistic activity only when there is no alternative. To remain at this level of activity is a sure guarantee of political impotence.

As a first step towards tackling the problems of sectionalism, it is necessary to distinguish four kinds of unity. The first is the unification of those involved in production, both by extending the trade union movement to unorganised workers and by unifying trade unions themselves, not institutionally, but to a common purpose. This latter task is often ignored; the degree to which British unions remain divided amongst themselves, is a source of constant weakness not to mention embarrassment. The second is the unification of all areas of social struggle, whether located in production or in other areas of social conflict. This precludes the erection of false barriers which classify various struggles into compartments, but rather requires that their common features be drawn out and emphasised. The third is the unifying of the political forces of the left. This is something we discuss below, but it should be clear that no left group has established any right to leadership or primacy. Fourth, and incorporating all these aspects of unity is the need to establish a national unity around a perspective of socialism. The concept of nationality is very difficult and cannot be considered here. It is unlikely, however, that socialism will be achieved unless it can in some way be identified with that body of historical sentiment called nationality. The balance between nationalism and internationalism has been very hard for socialists to find in the past. Rigid ideals of proletarian brotherhood have often in the past been swamped by spurious appeal to national unity (for example over the Common Market) or confused with the policies of the Soviet Union. Yet at some point, acceptable national feeling and socialism have to be balanced and merged.

2. National, Sexual and Racial Self-Determination

The second policy theme, which must be considered as functioning alongside the first, is the recognition of rights of self-determination for social and national groupings. Unity of any kind is spurious if it is based on any form of social oppression, and it must be recognised that most working class institutions are implicitly oppressive, sexually and racially. The right of any sexual, cultural or racial group to determine its own form of organisation has to be conceded to achieve any unity not rooted in deceit. This is not something which can be resolved without tensions or conflict, but the issues cannot be ignored or cloaked in organisational straitjackets. It is a difficult equation and one that can only be resolved by the next point.

3. The Extension of Democracy

This, the third policy theme, is the extension of democracy and self-management into all spheres of life. We have already stressed that bourgeois democracy cannot be regarded as a sham, but on the contrary is the most fundamental and progressive political advance achieved by capitalism. The object of socialist policies should not be to destroy or limit these advances but rather to develop and transend them by struggling for democracy in all spheres of society. The inherent limitations of bourgeois democracy are clear; it is indirect and does not extend to areas of everyday existence either at work or in social communities. It is in many cases, factured, debased and manipulated. Socialist democracy would be the reverse of this; it would be direct and ensure control over immediate issues without any intermediate manipulation or bureaucratic deformation. That at least is the intent. It is a severe handicap to any socialist, Communist or not, that the major international examples of allegedly "socialist" democracy are no more than perversions of this ideal.

The most important political contradiction of British society is that the very flexibility and resilience of bourgeois procedures has increasingly highlighted those major areas and issues, from workers' participation and urban redevelopment to the social responsibilities of science, in which these procedures are inadequate or a facade for authoritarian control. Socialist policies must insert the practice of genuine socialist democracy into these areas in a direct challenge to bourgeois forms.

One important corollary of this is that the formation and application of socialist policy must also be democratic. The labour movement in Britain has always contained an authoritarian and undemocratic strand; this applies equally to political groups and to trade unions. Socialists have never fully disengaged from the idea that the authoritarian structures can be captured and used by the left, and that this forms a short cut around the laborious process of democratic advance.

4. *Popular Mobilisation*

Fourth, and as an important adjunct to this last point, socialist policy must contain the potential for mobilising mass support at times of political crisis. This derives from the process of democratic involvement mentioned above but goes beyond it insofar as it requires a constant need to review the mechanisms and organisations by which policy is carried out. The greatest problem facing any socialist government is how to retain popular support through periods when measures of economic and financial stringency may be forced on it by the past policies of the capitalist governments or by external and internal economic blockade or sabotage. In past socialist revolutions, the practice has been to rely primarily upon physical coercion to sustain a socialist government in such circumstances. Areas and moments of physical violence may prove necessary in any British transition to socialism but this cannot be used as a major prop. The ability of the capitalist class to organise, finance and sustain physical repression at any required level is likely to outrun any parallel ability of socialists. The major defence of socialism must be the close and continuing support of the mass of the people, mobilised into effective public action.

5. *Policy as Real Intervention*

Fifth, socialist policy must contain an understanding of the contradictions of capitalist society and the way in which these may be used to deform and ultimately destroy capitalism. At the most abstract level, the basic contradiction of capitalism is the private ownership of social production, or, seen from a different angle, that production is motivated by exchange rather than use.

These formulations express a general idea which embraces specific contradictions in all spheres of society. It is, however, wrong to suppose that such abstract characterisations suffice to determine these specific contradictions, or the way in which they develop as attempts are made to resolve them. We have argued that the anarchy of capitalism has been substantially modified by the need to stabilise the social context of private production. This process has generated new contradictions which are not necessarily resolved in favour of private production even when capitalism remains dominant.

As an illustration of the kinds of contradictions at work consider at the economic level the problem of inflation. Modern inflation has developed out of the reconstituted economic and political structure of post-war capitalism. The establishment of a managed economy, incorporating a vastly enlarged social and economic role for the state within the political framework of a liberal democracy, was the basis of post-war capitalist restabilisation. Within and through this system working class organisation was drawn into the corporate functioning of capitalism. The unavoidable consequence has been the willingness and ability of the working class to press its claims over resources in the endless distributive struggle which is the essential driving force of inflation. This is a very broad encapsulation of the issue of inflation and does not pretend to analyse its full complexity. Yet it does show how in conceding the post-war settlement the ruling class delivered up a major hostage to fortune, and laid the basis for the most persistent and intractable post-war economic problem.

In the political sphere, we have already noted the contradiction of a form of democracy developed to assign limited and indirect control to the working class, but now confronted by social conflicts which demand full and direct control. At the ideological level, we can see the acute contradictions brought about by the need to reconcile the ideology of free enterprise, of private endeavour and private failure, with a society in which the scope of social regulation and responsibility has been steadily extended.

These are not illusory problems. We emphasised above that the active formation and consolidation of bourgeois hegemony is not a matter of the skilful propagation of lies but involves real intervention. Such intervention may itself give rise to contradictions, but the main characteristic of bourgeois hegemonic policies is usually just this attempt to control and channel contradiction. It follows that the socialist policy alternatives must also be *real* in the sense of not simply being an exercise of propaganda. To use a controversial example, to which we shall return, the development of incomes policies is an attempt to control inflationary contradictions by stepping up to a higher degree the incorporation of the working class into the functioning of a capitalist state. To call for a return to "free collective bargaining" and to expose such incomes policies as "fake" does not answer the *real* problem involved. "Free collective bargaining" represents no more than a stage of working class incorporation which itself causes the problem of inflation. To state the issue so boldly does not provide the correct alternative, but it does illustrate that formulating a correct socialist policy requires a greater understanding of real contradictions than much current left policy contains.

6. *The Growth of Socialist Relations within Capitalism*

Sixth, policy must be developed in a perspective of socialism. That is to say, it must not only *be*

socialist in the sense of proclaiming socialism as its
goal, but must also be clearly part of a process of
change *leading* to a socialist society. The most
fundamental mistake of previous Marxist practice
has been to assume that a clear and obvious gap
separates capitalism and socialism, with the implication that current policies need have no more
than a sloganistic connection with a future socialist
society. For example, immediate demands centre
around acquisitive gain whilst socialist perspectives
reject acquisitiveness; a future socialist society
would offer full democratic control, but immediate
demands for limited control are denounced as class
collaboration. Such a clear-cut distinction is at
least consistent if it is combined with a belief in a
single revolutionary transition defining the change
from capitalism to socialism. But if this latter idea
is rejected in favour of a process of political change
— as we believe it should be — then this process has
to be reflected in all immediate policy.

Moreover such a political process should not be
conceived of as commencing at some indeterminate
date in the future. Still less can it be considered as
only starting from the moment when programmatic
statements are articulated. Just as capitalism
predated *Das Kapital* so the process of achieving
socialism began before Eurocommunism. The
problem of how socialist relations can grow within capitalism is not easy, particularly if they
are given social, economic and cultural, as well as
simply political, dimensions. But the difficulties
have to be overcome. The process of achieving
socialism cannot be reduced to the building of a

political alliance; this is an exact parallel to the view that reduces hegemony to an exercise in political propaganda.

7. The Struggle against Social and Environmental Impoverishment

Seventh, all socialist policy must incorporate dimensions which help to enrich individual relationships between people and the relation between people and their environment. Such objectives are enshrined in particular political and social movements, but they transcend specific demands. Relative to pre-capitalist modes of production capitalism has greatly expanded the scope of social control and individual freedom. The sway of disease, ignorance and material deprivation has been pushed back; secular and humane values have advanced. But, as Marxists have always stressed, these achievements co-exist with the disintegrative ravages of market forces, the social division and personal misery caused by hierarchical domination and the brutalisation of the environment in which human activity is conducted.

The neglect of these aspects in favour of a crude materialism has been a constant flaw of socialist policy. An obvious example of this is housing policy; what should be one of the great achievements of post-war Britain, the transformation of private slums to publicly owned houses and flats has been sadly reduced by a failure to attend to the natural and social environment. The barren wastes of the new urban satellite housing estates, the tower-block scandal, the clear-and-build mentality

rather than renovation and preservation, have
marked out public housing as the refuge of the
oppressed rather than as any image of the future.
That counts as a mark against socialism which
recurs every time people mentally equate socialism
with the crude, the ugly and the second-rate.
And to refuse to believe that people make such
equations and adjust their political actions accor-
dingly has unfortunately been another mark of
past socialist practice.

8. Flexibility and Openness

A final theme is more of a party political lesson to
which we shall return in the next chapter. We have
enumerated a series of elements which must
permeate socialist policy; their complexity and
breadth of application are obvious. Any political
party which wishes to cope with this must learn
flexibility and openness as its only dogma. This
does not mean that there is no place for discussion
of guiding principles, still less that party political
activity should be liquidated into movements of
social protest and reform. The need for a clear,
firm set of principles remains as great as ever. The
point is that contemporary socialist politics neces-
sitates a thorough re-assessment and overhaul of
those modes of thought, organisation, practice and
style which the left has inherited from the past. No
British political group can look with sufficient
pride at its record over the last twenty years to
assert that it has yet learnt this lesson.

Economic Policy

It is quite impracticable to consider all areas of

policy in the light of these general principles; the task is too large and our own knowledge too limited. We should like to explore one particular topic – economic policy – because it corresponds to our own interests. This does not mean that economic issues are necessarily primary. One of our main points is that a *socialist* economic policy, as distinct from an economic policy which happens to be put forward by socialists, cannot be limited to the application of certain technical economic controls. What marks it out as socialist is that it forms part of a total project of social transformation.

A major criticism of much of the left's emphasis in economic matters is that it places too much weight on technical issues and measures. By 'technical' we mean measures which by themselves have no political bias and can be applied by the right as well as by the left. Measures such as nationalisation or import controls, which we discuss further below, do not contain any ingrained socialist content. If both the left and its opponents suppose that they *are* inherently socialist, it is due to force of habit and the political complexion of those who normally advocate these measures. But by taking for granted the political character of what in general amount to technical, apolitical controls, the left lays itself open to a number of problems.

One of these is that it is always open to a centre or right wing government to pre-empt the left, whenever political pressure mounts, by some suitable adaptation of left economic policy. Right wing governments are quite capable of applying strict controls on the export of capital without in any way conceding the socialist *objectives* which such controls could be used to help achieve.

Perhaps more important in the long term, the emphasis on technical controls tends to present a centralised and authoritarian image of socialism. Measures to prevent this and to limit that subject to government licence, re-inforce the widely held view of socialism as a system of bureaucratic repression.

Finally, excessive preoccupation with the technical aspects of economic policy can distract attention from its real social content. There is a tendency on the left to regard the 'siege' economy as an end in itself rather than as a debatably necessary step on the road to a fuller and freer socialism.

The Way Out of the Recession

Clearly the central feature of socialist economic policy is that it has to be applied in the context of the most stubborn and prolonged period of recession since the war. Three distinct factors have coincided to make the current recession particularly intractable. This point must be stressed: there is no simple socialist short cut to economic revival. Britain is too enmeshed with the world economy, and the root causes of industrial decline are too deep seated for that to be possible.

There is first the specific weakness of the British economy which we have already discussed. This prolonged relative failure has meant that the

British economy has become more vulnerable to international competition with a consequent loss of export markets and increased import penetration. It is clear that policy must focus on reversing this trend. What complicates the problem is that it now has to be tackled in an international context which is far more unfavourable than in the past.

The second factor is the world wide nature of the recession. For the first time since the war all the major capitalist economies have plunged into recession at the same time. Some tendency towards greater international synchronisation of cyclical fluctuations had already been set up in the 1960s because of the growing integration of European capitalism within the EEC, and of advanced capitalism generally through the progress of trade liberalisation and the role of the dollar and Eurodollar in world finance. But as long as the Bretton Woods international monetary system, remained in force, incorporating practically fixed exchange rates, this tendency was limited. Under fixed exchange rates deficit and surplus countries tend to maintain opposite policy stances — contractionary in the former case and expansionary in the latter. As the "discipline" of fixed exchange rates was gradually replaced by a regime of managed floating rates, separate economies were more liable to become locked into synchronised fluctuations. The OPEC price rises of 1973-4 finally clinched the process by subjecting all the advanced capitalist states to a common external shock. The contraction of national spending power caused by this sudden transfer of resources to the OPEC states, equivalent in most cases to 3-4% of GDP, drove them all into recession together. In addition the impact of the rise in oil prices on domestic rates of inflation, which were already running at immoderate levels by 1960s' standards, persuaded all governments that any attempt at stimulatory action to maintain output and employment, would cause an inflationary explosion. The only way in which the inflationary menace could be contained was by administering a rapid and, if necessary, prolonged deflationary jolt to capitalists and workers and allowing abnormal levels of unemployment and spare capacity to develop. This common fear of destabilising inflation accounts for the extreme caution of all governments towards the issue of restimulation, and the slow and faltering nature of the recovery which has been under way in 1976-7.

The synchronised pattern of recession together with the fact that the conflict between unemployment and inflation is everywhere more acute than in the 1960s, leaves world capitalism without a major dynamic economy capable of bailing out the rest with a growing export market. International negotiations have so far failed to achieve any measure of co-ordinated reflation.

This has been the most important failure qualifying the otherwise successful development of international capitalist negotiation and co-operation on trade and finance.

In the strong and previously fast-growing economies of Germany and Japan, capitalists have adjusted to the prospects of much lower future growth by severely curtailing their investment, hitherto a larger component of national income in these countries than elsewhere. With policy dominated by principles of 'sound' finance and of the liberal state, the resulting demand deficiency has not been offset by rising government expenditure. Personal consumption has also remained flat as insecure workers and members of the middle class increased their savings. Since the competitive strength of the German and Japanese economies remains substantially intact, their depressed internal state has allowed large trade surpluses to accumulate, which, in turn, have inhibited growth in the weaker states like Italy, France and Britain. The USA has experienced a modest internal expansion in the recent past, but its delay in curbing its energy consumption and its loss of competitiveness in some sectors have driven its balance of payments into deficit. The official remedy of a controlled devaluation of the dollar has disturbed international money markets, which as we have seen, have been held together by a process of rolling crisis management, rather than by any major reform of the international monetary system. Consequently anxieties about a recovery in the 'real' economies of the major capitalist states have been compounded by renewed fears of financial instability.

Recovery would probably be less sluggish if the recession were not marked by a third factor. This is the emergence of important structural problems within each of the advanced capitalist states. Postwar economic growth has been accompanied by a rapid expansion of trade in manufactured goods between developed capitalist countries and a similarly rapid expansion of demand for such goods within each country. Cars and consumer durables are the obvious examples.

It is evident that trade expansion, at rates twice or more than national growth rates, must eventually slow down if only because there are limits to the proportion of economic goods and services which are tradeable. More importantly, the demand for durable manufactured products tends to slow down as replacement rather than new purchase becomes the rule. This process has reached an advanced state for a number of staple manufactures of the post-war boom. Cars, household 'white' goods and TV sets are examples. As a result, national economies are facing problems of shifting human and capital resources into new growth areas. The coincident energy problem, (accelerated by the OPEC price rises, but based on genuine, long term natural resource constraints), also creates structural problems related to the level and form of energy consumption.

It is premature to talk of a 'post-industrial' society, that is a society in which the manufacturing sector forms only a small part of the economy and most human activity is directed towards the service sector. But this must be considered a likely future trend. This means that the present stagnation and decline of industries such as steel and shipbuilding is likely to continue. More generally, these structural trends suggest that there is little prospect that future growth can be mainly extensive, involving no more than the enlargement of the economy within its existing sectoral proportions.

There is no reason to believe that the decline within manufacturing of its post-war staples, or of manufacturing as a whole relative to services, implies overall economic stagnation. It is frequently either false or misleading to describe services as technically stagnant, as if restaurants and hair-dressing were typical of the disparate activities classified under the blanket heading of services. The point is that any serious socialist programme for economic expansion has to become integrated with a programme for economic restructuring of a larger magnitude, and involving correspondingly larger breaks with traditional socialist priorities, values and habits of thought, than have been confronted in the past. Any notion that Britain can simply replicate the past growth experience of the successful capitalist countries is an anachronistic delusion.

The combination of these three factors in the current recession means that British economic policy cannot be reduced to any simple recipe.

One strand of left wing thought holds that a left government could shrug off the international and structural constraints which we have described, by erecting barriers against imports and controls over international money flows so as to create a "siege economy". It is argued that in the short run import controls could stave off factory closures. In the medium run they would permit domestic expansion to reduce overall unemployment without a con-comitant deterioration in the balance of payments. In the long run they would provide a protective shield behind which the process of improving British industry's international competitiveness and restructuring the economy could be pursued through state intervention.

In the context of opposition to those who would consign Britain's destiny to the invisible hand of the world market, it is undoubtedly correct to press for an active, forward looking state industrial policy. Selective import controls would probably be an adjunct of such a policy. Presumably they would have to be in the form of quotas accompanied by a physical rationing system and a programme for expanding and improving locally produced substitutes, and not in the form of tariffs, which simply redirect market forces and provide no stimulus to revitalise stagnant industrial sectors. But import controls offer no panacea for escaping from the present recession. Their use is severely limited by three main problems.

The first is that diminished international competitiveness is an across the board problem affecting all main sectors of British industry. It is hard to imagine any economy-wide system of protection being feasible. This is closely related to the second issue, that of retaliation by trading partners. This cannot be simply brushed aside. Widespread import controls could not be unilaterally introduced without inviting a severe disruption of trading relations leading possibly to external embargo and other forms of international pressure. Import quotas for specific commodities would have to be internationally negotiated and this process would involve hard and lengthy bargaining. It would of

course be an important objective of a left government to work towards a greater measure of control
over the anarchy of international trade in the
form of bilateral or multilateral long term trade
agreements with other states, whether advanced
capitalist, socialist or developing. But no quick
results would be expected from this. In the short
to medium run, which is the natural timescale for
anti-recession policies, the best that could be
hoped for from international negotiations would
probably be the formation of a coalition of weak
states to use the threat of co-ordinated import
restrictions as a means of pressurising the strong
states into greater reflation. This, if successful,
would be no negligible achievement. It would
mark an important step towards curbing the
anarchy of the international economy through the
co-ordination of national demand management
policies.

The third difficulty with import controls is that
the phrase "siege economy", embraced with
enthusiasm by some sections of the left, betrays
a complete indifference to popular sensibilities.
Austerity measures, which were accepted in
conditions of wartime emergency, are unlikely to
recommend themselves to a population which has
grown accustomed to the freedom to opt for
imported products where these are cheaper or
of better quality than locally produced alternatives. Moreover, the attempt to control consumer
expenditure from the supply side, as in the USSR,
has generally proved to be cumbersome and
inefficient.

The fact is that in any economy which retains a substantial sector of market based industry and a large volume of private consumption expenditure, one of the major tools of policy will continue to be the manipulation of overall national demand through taxation or public expenditure. Although the major use of this tool has historically been that of sustaining equilibrium in capitalist economies, it is not a specifically capitalist instrument and is a legitimate and necessary part of any socialist economic policy. Attempts to replace Keynesian methods of economic management by automatic monetary controls are, as we have argued, fundamentally anti-democratic and reactionary. The tendency to write off Keynesian policies, which is common amongst Marxists, serves to reinforce this trend and has no basis other than in illusions about capitalist collapse.

The upshot of this argument is that in the short to medium term at least, the pace of economic expansion in Britain will have to be largely governed by the pace of economic expansion in the major capitalist economies. Over the longer term there is more freedom for manoeuvre and policy must be directed towards the independent revitalisation of British industry. Meanwhile attempts at sudden and large scale reflation would inevitably result in high import levels, inflation and exchange rate problems which could not be coped with by import and capital controls without provoking international retaliation and domestic unrest. The only recourse would then be to an equally abrupt reversal of expansion which would leave any

government ~~~~~~~~~~~~~~~~~~~~~~~~ uins and
ensure its p~~~~~~~~~~~~~~~~~~~~~~~

Incomes Poli

Britain has a ~~~~~~~~~~~~~~~~~~~~~ ation of
incomes poli~~~~~~~~~~~~~~~~~~~~ country
outside of Sc~~~~~~~~~~~~~~~~~ Netherlands. There
have been only a few years in the past fifteen when
the government of the day has not sought to exert
some form of direct control over the movement of
prices and money incomes. In part this has merely
been a consequence of the critical condition of
British capitalism over this period. But it also
testifies to the advanced state which the socialising
tendencies characteristic of post-war capitalism
have attained in Britain. Neither of these aspects of
incomes policy has been properly recognised by
the left and used to achieve political advance.

The issues can best be set out by examining the
Social Contract. This has been widely rejected
by the left as a corporatist confidence trick. In
explicitly agreeing to two successive rounds of
voluntary pay restraint and in acquiescing in a
third, it is argued, the trade union movement has
provided an indispensable prop to the strategy of
capitalist restabilisation, has compromised its
autonomy and defused the combative potential of
the working class. Only through resistance to
further rounds of pay restraint and a resumption of
normal collective bargaining can these self-imposed
afflictions be cast aside.

There are two decisive weaknesses in this position.

One is a straightforward consequence of the depressed condition of the British economy and its slow underlying rate of growth. The other stems from an assessment of the positive features of economy-wide pay agreements between the government and the trade union movement in the process of winning socialist hegemony.

The Economics of Pay Restraint

In the current economic situation the defeat of the Social Contract would be a Pyrrhic victory. At the economic level the force of this assessment depends on what assumption is made about the movement of money wages in the absence of any agreed pay ceiling. One assumption is that the abandonment of a formal incomes policy will make little overall difference. Alternatively it may be assumed that the restoration of normal collective bargaining will unleash a major wages offensive.

Current experience suggests that the former assumption is more realistic. The movement of average earnings did not greatly exceed the official 10% ceiling of Phase 3 despite the greater flexibility allowed for pay rises in the private sector than in the previous two phases. Nevertheless the latter assumption remains a possibility to be reckoned with. Acceptance of the pay policy has been increasingly reluctant and bitter. The multiple grievances and resentments which have accumulated, but remain latent, during the worst of the slump could erupt in a pay revolt if market conditions move in labour's favour.

Consider the first prospect. It is arguable that a

combination of high unemployment, monetary discipline and reductions in taxation will keep money wage settlements down to modest overall proportions. In this case the only major consequence of a return to normal collective bargaining would be to introduce greater flexibility for individual bargaining units and allow some widening of previously compressed pay differentials. There is certainly scope for such readjustments. Private sector profitability has recovered slightly from the low point reached in 1975. Similarily in the public sector, the overkill policy applied to public spending over the last two years now provides a margin of slack to accommodate pay increases and pay restructuring for employees of central and local government.

As the public sector unions realise, however, their bargaining space is narrowly circumscribed by the continuing pressure for curbs on social spending. If they are to be subject to pay restraints via cash limits, they have every interest in preserving an incomes policy in order to prevent their pay deteriorating relative to the private sector and in order to keep down the rate of inflation.

Such fine distributive calculations are the very stuff of normal collective bargaining. But a perspective of wringing the maximum practicable sectoral wage concessions out of employers within the narrow limits set by the prevailing harsh economic environment, scarcely amounts to a socialist crusade. It may be objected that if workers are not engaged in sectoral wage struggles they will not be prepared to struggle for wider objectives either. This traditional view, with a pedigree dating back to Marx and Engels, has some truth for the formative stages of capitalist development or for groups of workers with no background of union organisation and struggle. What it ignores are the ambiguous social functions of wages and conditions bargaining once it has become normalised. It is an arena within which class struggle is continually mobilised and *at the same time contained*. For example, collective action to influence the terms on which labour power is exchanged helps to overcome the most elementary obstacle to class unity — that of pure individualism. But because bargaining is structured on sectional lines it acts as a barrier to the achievement of higher levels of collectivity. Similarly the wages struggle offers a channel for the expression of felt material deprivation, but in the process confirms and re-inforces the economic and social structures of contemporary mass consumption. A reversion to normal collective bargaining represents a retreat from the difficult task of finding ways of resolving these ambiguities. The relevance of a socialist contract to this task is discussed below.

Consider now the consequences of a wages offensive. This is usually advanced as part of a comprehensive alternative economic programme. Its advocates appreciate that in an economy whose real output is undergoing negligible growth, a major upsurge in wages would inevitably cause disruption if it were not complemented by more far-reaching measures. In order to fix ideas it is worth spelling out in some detail the chain reactions which a wages push would set in motion.

There is first the "confidence" effect on the behaviour of foreign and domestic capitalists. Apart from the familiar outburst of political hysteria the most immediate economic manifestation would be a rapid fall in the exchange rate with subsequent repercussions on import prices which would feed into industrial and living costs. Foreign central banks would agree to support the exchange rate only if the government took steps to restore domestic order. Whether this kind of pressure is described as blackmail or as the rational pursuit of class interest is immaterial. It remains a major point of vulnerability. If, as both historical experience and reflection on contemporary reality suggest, such pressure is unlikely to be effectively countered by voluntaristic appeals to stand firm or by the imposition of a state of siege, it would be better to avoid entering this particular battle in the first place.

Suppose one discounts the prospect of external destabilisation. There remains the internal sequence of reactions. As large rises in money wages drive up unit costs either the profitability of capitalist and public enterprises falls, or they raise prices, or some combination of the two. The balance between these outcomes would depend on the intensity of price competition between capitalists, and on the general policy stance of the state towards inflation as reflected in the pricing policies of the nationalised industries, the state's willingness to allow the exchange rate to depreciate and the outlook for total demand. The state would face a choice

between making offsetting cuts in its total expenditure as previously projected expenditure ceilings
were breached, or relieving this pressure by allowing
its total expenditure to rise above planned targets.
In the latter case the excess would have to be
financed by some combination of higher taxes,
higher borrowing from the non-bank public and a
faster growth of the money supply. Each of
these options would produce its own complex
repercussions on the course of inflation.

If the state were prepared to ratify a wage-led
increase in the rate of inflation by adopting a
generally permissive stance on policy, the result
would indeed be faster inflation. To defend their
real incomes workers and other social groups
would be forced to step up their monetary claims.
The spiral would continue indefinitely and almost
certainly accelerate in pace as attempts to anticipate
future inflation began to exert an influence on
wage settlements, pricing policies and consumer
behaviour. Since rampant inflation is profoundly
socially destabilising sooner or later one of the
links in the inflationary chain would be broken,
whether by the re-introduction of an incomes
policy or the reversal of the state's permissive
demand policy.

In contemporary Britain it is almost certain that
a government which permitted an acceleration of
inflation for any length of time would fall. Inflation
is widely feared and resented particularly after the
unprecedented wage-price spiral of 1975, which led
directly to the first phase of pay restraint under
the Social Contract. It is important to remember

that the Social Contract did not originally involve an incomes policy. Moreover the ground for a tough stand on public expenditure and monetary restraint has by now become well established, and commands a wide measure of popular support. It is therefore inevitable that having rejected the direct discipline of pay restraint, the unions would find themselves subjected to the traditional, indirect discipline of rising unemployment as the combination of wages offensive and monetary counter-offensive increased the rate of bankruptcies, lay-offs and redundancies. A sophisticated government could even turn the situation to ideological advantage by deploying the seductive logic of free choice: unions and workers should not be *coerced* into pay settlements, but should *choose* their preferred combination of inflation and unemployment. Whether and at what eventual level of unemployment the rate of wage and price increases could be beaten down by this painful route would depend on how stern a disciplinarian the state was prepared to be and on the responses of capitalists, workers and unions. What is certain is that neither the interim acceleration in inflation nor the accompanying rise in unemployment would be in the interests of the working class.

The left's counter to this grim scenario is to invoke alternative policies which would interrupt the chain of events. Thus it is suggested that a left government could stem the tide of price rises at source by introducing a six month price freeze followed by stringent price controls. In the context of a wages offensive such a policy would force capitalists into bankruptcy or evasion of the controls. Either way, in the ensuing crisis the government would acquire an excuse for further intervention in the private sector leading to outright public ownership. Similarly it is recommended that the spillover from higher real wages and higher private consumer spending into higher imports should be averted by the speedy implementation of sweeping controls over international trade and finance. In short current left policy envisages the economic equivalent of storming the barricades.

The paradox of this romantic vision is that a simple economic advance — a short run increase in real wages — turns out to require for its realisation a more or less immediate transition to a fully socialised economy. The long standing problem of forging connections between immediate struggles and socialist objectives is resolved in this perspective by the expedient of running them together. Free collective bargaining becomes a subterfuge for a socialist transformation.

The Politics of Pay Restraint

The analysis so far has centred on the limitations inherent in a purely corporate-defensive working class economic policy and the patent unrealism of left attempts to graft on to this a perspective for socialist advance. The problem remains, however, of how to effect a linkage between socialist objectives of planning and social control on the one hand and the historical experience and contemporary practice of trade unionism on the other.

It is moreover virtually axiomatic that trade union autonomy and the right to use collective strength in order to influence and change government policy, even at the cost of economic disruption, must be retained in the process of socialist transition. What the left has failed to appreciate is that the general principle of a social contract, as distinct from the Labour Government's current degenerated pay policy, offers a way out of the impasse of trade union economism, which both engages with the existing practice of collective bargaining and is compatible with established freedoms.

In principle a social contract is nothing more than an economy-wide agreement between the government and the trade union movement under which rules are drawn up to regulate pay settlements within lower level bargaining units in return for an explicit commitment by the government to a particular set of economic and social policies. Considered as an ongoing institution this is a form of collective bargaining conducted at the level of the economy as a whole. Negotiation at this level falls by definition within the domain of politics since the terms under negotiation are the policy of the state itself. Nevertheless a social contract recognisably belongs to the same species as more familiar modes of collective bargaining. In principle it involves no greater or smaller compromise of trade union autonomy of organisation and action than any other collective agreement. A particular agreement may be more or less unfavourable to the unions. As long as the contract remains on a voluntary basis, the unions remain free to press for a revision of the terms, or, for that matter, to refuse to enter any agreement at all and revert to exclusive reliance on normal collective bargaining.

It is this feature of a social contract which provides the link with the experience and traditions of the trade union movement. It is accepted that union objectives and tactics in normal wage bargaining take into account such plant, enterprise or industry level factors as productivity, profitability and employment levels as well as more general factors such as the past, and perhaps anticipated future, movement of the cost of living. (Pay relativities involve separate considerations such as comparative levels of skill, training, effort, responsibility and working conditions). A social contract involves an extension of this list to include the appropriate equivalent factors at the macro-economic level. It is true that the inter-relations between macro-economic variables — aggregate wages, productivity, prices, profits, taxes, the money supply, output, employment, the exchange rate, the terms of trade, etc. — are remote from popular consciousness, complex and disputed. But this merely complicates the enlargement of the context of collective negotiations; it does not invalidate it. Union negotiators from shop stewards upwards are perfectly accustomed to handling equally complex and contentious issues at the micro level, when the repercussions of current actions for the future have to be carefully weighed and sectional interests equilibrated. The attainment of a similar degree of familiarity and fluency with macro level issues is a natural development, already under way in some sections of the movement. Moreover any realistic prospect of transition to democratic socialist economic planning depends on the further growth of the trade union movement's directive capacity and the strengthening of articulation between workplace and national levels.

At the same time a social contract introduces a definite break with the past. This is not because an agreed set of pay norms is by definition an attempt to impose conscious social regulation on the characteristic anarchy of pay determination under capitalism and the associated distribution of income both between and within classes. This is a feature of any incomes policy. The novel element of a social contract is the principle that the trade unions should not accept or be expected to accept responsibility for the performance of the economy without a corresponding extension of power to influence national policy. The witholding of corporate economic strength on the wages front becomes conditional on, and therefore a vital means of achieving, social and political advance.

This quid pro quo principle presents a major opportunity for subverting capitalism by linking the issues of pay and inflation with those structural issues — the volume, pace and composition of investment, the pattern of production and consumption, the scale, direction and composition of foreign trade, the character and consequences of technical innovation — which under capitalism are determined anarchically as the outcome of private action and decision beyond the scope of

a social contract
he assertion of a
for the national
shifting the terms
of ther a progressive
soc

T exchange of quid for quo are
precisely the familiar risks of collective bargaining
in general. The trade union leadership may be
outmanoeuvred or subdued by superior force.
The process of matching concessions on pay for
concessions on policy may easily degenerate into
a hard headed corporatist exercise in the mutual
adjustment of demands which accept and confirm
the social and economic status quo. It is also
evident that the progressive potential of a social
contract will be fully realised only under a left
government. But there is no reason in principle
why the *attempt* to realise this potential should
not be made whatever government is in office. The
political value of a social contract lies as much in
the going as in the arriving. The risks involved are
real and must be faced. But to reject the principle
because of these risks is to condemn the working
class to a permanent role of defiant subordination
to bourgeois hegemony.

Those who argue that the acceptance of the
present Social Contract has been the mainstay of
the Labour Government's overall strategy for
restabilising and over the long run restructuring
British capitalism have already unwittingly conceded this case. For whether a temporary sacrifice
of economic power by the working class becomes

transmuted in   pitalist
dominance is n   mined
by the unmov   ver. It
depends crucia   rategy
and policy of   ognise
and utilise the   ystem
of bourgeois he

Objections to a Socialist Social Contract

There are two arguments used against the adoption
by socialists of an incomes policy of the type we
have discussed.

The first amounts to a strategic rejection of the
entire perspective which we have advanced throughout this essay. Any involvement by the working
class in the functioning of capitalism is condemned
outright. The wages struggle is regarded as an
important, perhaps *the* important, arena for
provoking a confrontation with the ruling class and
the state. The defeat of incomes policies is viewed
as a political, as well as an economic victory. Any
adverse economic effects caused by the failure of
an incomes policy are considered to derive from
the internal 'crisis' of capitalism for which the
working class has neither any responsibility nor any
solution, other than the destruction of capitalism.

We disagree profoundly with this approach, but
it should be clear that our disagreement runs right
across the spectrum of political action and policy:
it is not confined to the specific topic of an incomes
policy. Those who stand by the classic Marxist
tradition of a single decisive revolutionary confrontation in the political sphere have every reason

to regard their opposition to incomes policies as consistent with their general political attitudes. The inconsistency lies with those who claim to accept the perspective of socialist gradualism in the political and social spheres, but try to erect some strategic opposition to it at the economic level. Those who believe in a gradual shift from a capitalist 'now' to a socialist 'then' are obliged to elaborate how they envisage this shift developing in *all* areas of society. And as any feasible form of socialism will involve the planning of personal consumption, at least at the aggregate level and if only as the obverse of planning investment, there is no alternative but to propose the gradual development of an incomes policy. It is possible to argue for the tactical postponement of such a policy on the basis of considerations about working class maturity. But it is hopelessly inconsistent to argue for a principled and strategic rejection of *all* incomes policies as a supposed way of developing that maturity.

We have argued this in relation to incomes policies but the same conflict exists in other areas of economic policy. We can note for example the apparent inability of many who accept political gradualism to come to terms with the issue of workers' control in industry as other than a demand to be achieved *after* the political victory of socialism and not as a stage in achieving that victory. The question of an incomes policy emerges not as some distasteful side-issue best not mentioned, even by those who doubt the wisdom of the current reflex response of the left. Rather it is a vital threshold which has to be surmounted before *any* consistent left economic policy can be advanced. It is for this reason that we have devoted so much space to the issue.

The tactical argument, which is the second objection raised against our position, is also difficult to sustain in practice, even though it may be formally consistent with a belief in political gradualism. The claim often made is that opposition to incomes policy is so deeply ingrained in the British trade union movement, that any change of position by the left would prove demoralising. This may or may not be true; opposition is certainly ingrained in the British left, but the left's inability to win any secure basis for mass leadership may well be connected with its tendency to transfer its own opposition to the bulk of trade union members. But even if the claim is justified the position of tactical resistance to incomes policy is difficult to raise above the level of Micawber's oportunism: that next year something will turn up and that the issue of incomes policy will go away. For better or for worse this is not very likely. A long term commitment to a socialist incomes policy will *have* to be formulated in the middle of opposing a short term capitalist policy. This may be an incomes policy; it may be some kind of monetarism. In either case resort to a socialist incomes policy will be tactically difficult. This task will never become easier as the years pass and it will always be possible to raise tactical objections to jumping the strategic hurdle.

It is undoubtedly true that the existing Social

Contract had degenerated. Its terms had been fudged to the point where its appeal rested on little more than a weary and increasingly fragile loyalty to Labour combined with narrow haggling over tax concessions. The Government's strategy for export growth and a recovery in private investment relied essentially on the operation of market forces and private capitalist initiative. State intervention was confined to rationalisation within public enterprise, specific tax and other measures to improve profitability, and the creation of a general climate of confidence. This dependence on the existing balance between public and private economic power left Britain's economy and society bereft of clear and purposeful national leadership. It reduced ultimately to a perverse act of faith in the dynamic capacity of British capital to reverse Britain's historic decline. The result was a gross and dangerous imbalance between the immediate reality of sacrifice and the remote prospect of reward, which had devalued the terms of the Social Contract, jeopardised its chance of survival and squandered its progressive potential.

The responsibility for this bleak outlook lies as much with the failures and weaknesses of the left as with the sins and strengths of the Labour leadership. The left's failure to transcend the twin perspectives of economism and romantic revolutionism parallels and sustains the continued tenure of social democratic realism. On the specific issue of incomes policy the way forward from this impasse lies in a redirection of thought and struggle at all levels of the labour and progressive movement, from the workplace and community up to General Council of the TUC and the various structures of the Labour Party, towards the definition of the terms of a new socialist social contract.

Some clues and guidelines as to what such a redirection would involve can be found in the themes taken up in the Labour Party's 1973 Programme and its 1974 Election Manifesto. These centred on the role of the National Enterprise Board, the development of a system of planning agreements with leading private corporations and the democratisation of industrial policy formation and management. These issues are more fully discussed in the section on economic policy below. The point to be stressed in the present context is that these ideas contain the germ of a fully fledged programme around which, after Labour took office in 1974 the issue of the Social Contract could have been debated and negotiated and a progressive alliance mobilised. They offered a method of projecting into the centre of national political life as the conditions of any economy-wide pay agreement, the need for state intervention and an extension of working class power in order to resolve the persistent failures of British capitalism in the spheres of investment, innovation foreign trade and regional development, and in order to integrate industrial policy with social needs. The defeats and demoralisation which the left has suffered over the past three years serve only to emphasise the continuing necessity to develop these themes into a hegemonic economic strategy.

Public Expenditure

Public expenditure is one of the central political issues of our time. It is necessary to understand why it occupies such a central position and why policy concerning public expenditure has to be framed with great care.

The most obvious reason is the sheer volume of resources which are channelled through state agencies. Even that part of state expenditure which makes no direct claim on resources but transfers income from one section of society to another, has important repercussions for the distribution of income and the acceptance of social responsibility for problems of unemployment, illness and other causes of material deprivation.

It is however wrong to adopt a purely economic approach towards state expenditure policy. The recent onslaught against the public sector has not originated from economic causes, though it is true that a variety of spurious economic issues have been invoked to supply a rationale for the attack. These issues must be tackled for the nonsense they are. There is, for example, no evidence for the claim that Britain's budgetary deficit is larger than that of other, virtuous capitalist countries such as West Germany, nor that it has been larger than might have been expected at a time of high and rising unemployment. The belief that the state has pre-empted investment resources or caused the balance of payments deficit is equally unfounded. Nor is it true that the burden of taxation is significantly higher in Britain than elsewhere once account is taken of different arrangements for funding pension and health insurance.

But having rebutted these contentions, socialists must also come to terms with the real reason for the attack on public expenditure, which is the decisive social changes which is has engendered. Unless this is done there is a constant danger that some of the attack will be conceded. Indeed on one basic point, that state expenditure is 'unproductive' and 'non-wealth producing', there are signs that the concession has already been made. In general the left has been blind to the inherent relativism of any distinction between 'productive' and 'unproductive' economic activity. It has espoused with enthusiasm those latter day versions of the doctrines of the 18th century Physiocrats, which substitute manufacturing for agriculture as the ultimate source of the nation's wealth. In doing so the left has unwittingly lent its support to those reactionary forces who correctly perceive that the steady march of socialisation has profoundly disturbed the normal functioning of market mechanisms and its associated free enterprise and individualist ideology and who desire therefore to roll back the frontiers of state activity and to restore a "proper" relationship between state and market. The only sense in which manufacturing industry is "productive" whereas public services are not, is that within advanced capitalism manufacturing is the central stronghold of capitalist commodity production, the principal arena within which profits are generated and appropriated for private corporate use. Aside from this issue of ownership and the principles which regulate its functioning, there is no absolute sense in which a factory is productive whereas a hospital or a hotel are not. A hospital, a hotel and a factory are all capable of producing profits under private ownership. Equally they can all be run by the state for social ends. What counts as a contribution to total output, or is included in calculations of productivity, depends on what criteria are being used to measure performance.

The social significance of public expenditure can only be understood by referring to our previous discussion on modes of production. The state sector is the most important example of a mode within capitalist society which is not itself organised within capitalist relations of production. This statement does not by itself define the social function of state expenditure. That can only be done by reference to concrete conditions. What it does do is to focus attention on a particular set of problems, notably those concerned with the dominant and progressive nature of particular modes of production at particular points in history. In this context the state sector in Britain signifies the very advanced nature of Britain's social relations.

The point can be illustrated by a comparison of Britain's health service with those of other countries. There is a clear progression in the development of social responsibility for medicine, which, for convenience, can be divided into stages. In practice there have not usually been major discontinuities between one stage and the next, and elements of superseded stages tend to survive on the fringes of more advanced forms of organisation.

In the first stage medicine remains a private industry. Doctors charge patients directly and hospitals and other medical facilities are run for profits. Social responsibility for medicine is contained within the sphere of private charity. This basic level is now largely confined to the USA and a few underdeveloped countries with right wing governments. Even the USA is now undergoing the transition to the second stage.

In this stage private insurance against the costs of medical treatment, which grew up in the first stage, becomes regularised by the state and is made compulsory for increasingly wide sectors of the population by levies on employers as well as workers. In addition the state may assume a regulatory function with respect to charitable institutions and begins to supply certain types of medical facility, such as mental hospitals, itself. This stage characterises the medical services of a country like Germany. Here, in the wake of the Bismark reforms, almost everyone is covered by medical insurance, regulated by the state, but operated by a number of quasi-independent agencies.

In the third stage the state takes over the insurance system and nationalises most medical institutions. Individual doctors may remain outside the system and those within it may retain some formal independence, but the state becomes the direct employer of all other health workers. Finance may be provided by a separate compulsory insurance payment. This corresponds to the situation prevailing in Britain after 1945 and to the scheme which has been proposed, but not implemented, in Italy.

In the fourth stage, separate insurance payments are dropped and medical funds are provided out of general taxation. All medical workers, including doctors, tend to become state employees. This is the current situation in Britain, and in Britain alone, of all capitalist societies.

There is also a further stage not yet attained anywhere, but prefigured in the activities of those sections of the women's movement concerned with women's health and the organisation of medical care, and in the perspectives beginning to emerge within the health service trade unions, for the democratisation of the health service. This stage can be seen as emerging from a process of direct and conscious reconstruction of the relations of power, accountability and control, both within the health service and between the health service and the community. During this process the dominance and elitism of doctors and the remoteness of the medical bureaucracy would be eclipsed by a more egalitarian and pluralist set of relations between all sections of the health service labour force. At the same time, the service would itself become more closely geared towards and responsive to the various needs and interests of the patients.

It must be emphasised that this classification of stages refers only to the social status of the medical industry not the volume of resources devoted to it. A country like Germany subtracts by compulsory insurance a higher proportion of income than is implicity subtracted by taxation in this country to pay for its health services. The decisive difference lies in the social consequences and perceptions of these payments.

An interesting example, again drawn from the medical sphere, is the way in which doctors have been drawn into typical trade union activities to further their interests. Such action have now moved beyond the partly 'respectable', partly concealed restrictive practices by which doctors have defended their corporate interests in the past. Strikes by consultants and junior hospital doctors reflect, unwittingly, the nature of the medical services in which they now work. Doctors have not become 'workers' like everyone else; their social power and status and their relations both with other health workers and with patients rule out such a simplistic assessment. But their economic militancy does derive from the change in status brought about by the increasingly socialised nature of medicine.

Britain's state sector has in many areas ascended from a purely subordinate role to capitalist production — whether in the provision of direct services (for example the education of skilled workers), or in assisting the process of capitalist reproduction through stabilising capitalist social relations — and has acquired a much more independent and socially ambiguous role. This has created enormous hostility to the state sector, which finds its expression in ideological opposition to the erosion of various norms of bourgeois society. This can be seen very clearly in the current educational debate about the purpose of state education.

However, in addition to ideological opposition there is another, more legitimate stream of criticism of state activity, stemming from the bureaucracy and inertia which has developed within it. This tendency has various origins but an important one is the ambiguity which attends the functions of the state sector. Increasingly its required standards of performance contain a mixture of social and commercial guidelines. These are almost impossible to operate except within the bounds of a bureaucracy which lays down minute procedures lacking any justification or purpose outside the bureaucracy. The state sector has become not so much inefficient as devoid of any social standards of efficiency.

The fusion of these two strands, a genuine dislike of bureaucracy and an ideological resistance masked with economic rationality, has produced a dangerous and widely accepted conclusion: that the state sector is holding back the development of the productive forces by hogging resources and stifling initiative. The defence offered by socialist policy has tended to be defective on two crucial points. First, it has dodged the issue of public sector bureaucracy for fear of offending public sector unions. Second, it has remained equivocal in its attitude towards the state sector, regarding it on the one hand as a repressive instrument of bourgeois power, and on the other as the embodiment of moral rectitude. The result has been that socialist policy has rested on the shaky foundations of this moral stand and a general demand for economic expansion based on Keynesian public expenditure manipulations.

We believe that socialist policy on public expenditure should be far richer than this, incorporating in concrete form all the principles of policy we discussed above.

It should attempt to unify all workers around the issue, instead of driving an implicit wedge between them by accepting false distinctions between manufacturing industry and the public sector, and by discussing public spending as if its ultimate purpose were simply to provide jobs for teachers, health workers and so on. The emphasis must be on the nature and quality of the services provided. If it were shown that a given cut in social service spending could easily lead to a much greater proportionate deterioration in the service provided to the public, this would be better propaganda against the cuts and would help to restore morale among the forces of the left for whom nationalisation and public spending have long ceased to be objects of positive propaganda.

Policy must also recognise that particular sectional interests are not given enough freedom in the present system. For example the relations between schools and parents are often exclusive and authoritarian. Similarly the issue of democratic control over the public sector must be faced not just in terms of formal representation on committees, but in terms of an active relationship between public sector activities and the communities which they serve. For example the long

promised development of district health centres
must be accelerated despite the persistent oppos-
sition of local doctors.

Above all the state sector represents, and indeed
in many respects is, the embodiment of socialist
practice. No amount of Marxist rhetoric about how
different things will be in some future socialist
state alters the fact that the present functioning of
state activity determines popular attitudes to
socialism. Nor are popular perceptions entirely
wrong. There is, for example, a clear link between
the state bureaucracy of socialist countries and the
bureaucracies of our own local government. They
spring essentially from the same cause: that they
are administrative agents within an unresolved and
ambiguous mode of production which, lacking
any external referents, can only function under
internally imposed rules. The basic test of socialist
policy towards the public sector must always be:
what demonstration of socialist practice does a
particular policy supply? This is not always an easy
yardstick to apply and it is one which existing
policy often evades with the excuse that capitalism
must corrupt. But it is necessary.

Investment, Nationalisation and Planning

Investment, by general consensus, lies at the heart
of Britain's economic problems. An astonishing
spectrum of opinion, including the leaders of the
Labour and Conservative Parties, the CBI and the
TUC, the Communist Party and the Tribune Group
— in fact all informed opinion — agrees that British
needs 'more investment'. This consensus dissolves

when discussion turns to explanations and remedies.

The right argues that 'real', that is in their terms private, manufacturing investment has been starved by high taxation and union wage pressure, which have both eroded profitability. Blame is also directed at the state's permissive stand on inflation, which has disrupted business confidence, and at low industrial productivity which has depressed the return on investment. The proposed solution is to cut government expenditure, restrain private consumption and reduce and stabilise inflation. At the same time the unemployment level must cease to be a target and become an instrument of policy. A permanently higher margin of unemployment puts pressure on those in work to accept changes in working practices — line speeds, job times, manning ratios, demarcation rules — which will raise productivity on existing equipment and clear the way for the introduction of new equipment and technique.

The left has attributed low investment to the tendency of British capital to be invested overseas to the detriment of domestic industry and to speculation in land, real estate and commodities. If returns on investment are low, this is because of the cumulative effect of low levels of investment in the past. Attempts to regenerate industry by raising profitability will fail because there is no positive link in Britain's case between higher profits and higher investment. The proposed solution is for the state to intervene directly in manufacturing investment either by nationalisation or through such bodies as the NEB or by channelling the investment flows of the banks, pension funds and

insurance companies. As an adjunct to this programme the left advocates protective import
quotas and additional controls on the export of
capital.

Despite these differences of analysis and policy
what is striking is the congruence between these
positions with respect to the definition of the
problem to be tackled and the destination to be
aimed at. Both left and right share the assumption
that in some sense Britain's weakness stems from
its inadequate investment record, especially in
manufacturing, which as a result has grown anaemic
and now requires a major transfusion.

Socialist investment policy cannot, however,
afford any uncritical acceptance of prevailing
assumptions and categories. The dangers of this
have already been indicated in the discussion of
public expenditure. Consider first the issue of the
objectives to which investment is the means. Some
objectives virtually impose themselves on any
policy because of the inheritance of the past. Thus
any government confronts the need to regain
industrial competitiveness in order to place Britain's
visible trade balance on a sounder basis and thereby
remove a persistent constraint on the achievement
of full employment and faster growth. It is now
widely acknowledged that this objective cannot be
met solely by lowering the relative price of British
goods through currency depreciation and containing
domestic inflation. Policies operating only on price
competitiveness ignore the non-price elements of
competition, which become increasingly important
in markets for sophisticated, high technology

manufactures. Exclusive reliance on such policies in the past has kept British industries stuck 'down market', capable of producing only those low grade manufactures which have the least growth potential in world markets. Movement 'up market' requires a programme for modernising products and processes and for improving design, delivery times, after sales service, etc. Thus one important objective of investment policy is to promote this process of modernisation.

But this statement scarcely exhausts the content of a *socialist* investment policy. What has been absent from discussions on the left, or in any part of the political spectrum for that matter, is any systematic attention to long term objectives. Ultimately this turns on the kind of society which it is considered desirable and possible to build and work for. The left sometimes appears to favour a centrally planned equivalent of the successful capitalist states. This is a vision which conveniently ignores the social violence and environmental devastation which has been the price of, say, the Japanese economic miracle. It is of very limited use to speak of 'more investment' in the abstract. A blanket policy of building more roads, power stations, aircraft, computers, houses or any of the other items included in the disparate collection of hardware known as "gross fixed capital formation", for no better reason than to push the share of investment above some arbitrary figure, makes no sense to anyone. At some point one has to become specific about the composition of this bundle, and the purposes and consequences attached to it.

Nor is this issue of objectives a diversion from 'real' issues. In such recent controversies as the future of the car industry or the development of nuclear power, it has become apparent that a socialist policy is implausible unless it is rooted in the social and environmental context from which it is at present isolated.

The Chrysler rescue in 1976 epitomises the problem. The left's immediate policy demands for nationalisation and massive subsidy ran into trouble as many questioned the wisdom of extending the publicly owned sector of an industry faced with more than merely temporary problems of excess capacity. Moreover workers in other sectors must have been left wondering why car workers' jobs should be worth such subsidy when jobs elsewhere were disappearing fast. It is true that the left also dreams of an integrated transport system incorporating a nationalised automotive sector restructured towards production of public vehicles instead of private motor cars. But no such perspective informed immediate policy. The inevitable result of the compartmentalisation of immediate policy and long term perspectives is that in practice the long term issues are neglected or reserved for rare moments of tranquil contemplation.

The fact that these issues are so rarely discussed is due to the tendency of economists, to which the left has succumbed, to reduce Britain's investment problem to a matter of aggregative disproportions and technical difficulties. Accustomed by long years of habit to think of the transfer of political power as the capture of certain key state institutions, the left assumes that the key problem of investment is the centralisation of investible funds under state control. If failure lies in some overall shortfall of aggregate investment or some gross sectoral imbalance, then the remedy lies in grasping the technical levers of control, and questions such as where to invest, what criteria to employ and how to optimise the use of resources appear of secondary importance.

This investment strategy has three inherent defects. First there is no necessary reason to suppose that the government is an efficient allocator of funds. The debate over the relative advantages of central allocation and local initiative subjected to market forces is not irrelevant even within an economy in which the capitalist mode is dominant. There is no clear evidence that government-directed investment has in the past been more successful than that originating from decentralised decisions. This is notable in the energy sector which is almost totally dominated by government controlled investment, and in which government policy has successively almost ruined the coal, nuclear and generation industries. This is not to say that central planning has no role: simply that a correct balance has to be struck and that no one can be dogmatic about where that balance lies.

Second, the strategy has grave weaknesses with respect to the external relations of the British economy. Capital export is not a melodrama in which bags of pound notes are taken out of the country by shifty speculators. It is a much more

complicated matter bound up with repatriated
profits and the financing of overseas subsidiaries.
The export of capital by British companies is
already tightly controlled, though it is a weakness
of the control system that the committee which
vets applications for permission to transfer funds
is drawn only from the Bank of England and the
Treasury, and considers only the balance of payments implications of the applications it receives;
the re-investment of profits earned by overseas
subsidiaries or the raising of foreign capital escape
control. It is undoubtedly within the power of the
government to extend control over a wider area.
But it must be faced that such measures would
disrupt the inflow of foreign capital into Britain
in rather larger amounts than the outflow. The net
result would almost certainly be a drop in available
investment funds. Such a price may be judged
acceptable, but it is rarely made explicit in left
policy.

The third defect is that this strategy pays no
attention to the issue of productivity, particularly
in manufacturing. All the evidence suggests that
while there may be a small difference between
Britain and other countries in the proportion of
national income devoted to manufacturing investment, this disparity is slight by comparison with
the major difference in the productivity of investment. The years from 1950 to the early 1970s saw
the gap between Britain and the other advanced
states in terms of the share of investment gradually
reduced to the point where an increase of two or
three percentage points would have sufficed to

push Britain up to the average. This missing slice of investment may have been important for the economy's capacity for modernisation and innovation. But it does tell against the view that the problem of investment is *simply* one of aggregate volume. Moreover to the extent that there is an overall scarcity problem about investment, so that an increase in investment means less available in the short term for public or private consumption, this is a rather smaller problem than is often imagined. Such a comparatively minor shift as that required to raise Britain's investment ratio to a level that would stand comparison with most other capitalist powers, would entail little hardship and ought to be within the reach of the most casual of plans.

If the level and/or rate of growth of output per worker in British industry compares unfavourably with other countries, and if Britain's rise in output per unit of investment is significantly lower than elsewhere, the clear implication is that Britain's problems cannot be solved solely by increasing the proportion of resources devoted to investment. There is naturally a widespread reluctance to accept these arguments on the left. They are seen as opening the way to attacks on manning levels and trade union standards in the workplace. Immense energy is expended in trying to demonstrate that if low productivity exists it is due to outdated equipment or incompetent management, or alternatively that it is justified by the need to keep down stress and the risk of accidents at work.

But such a corporate defensive response is beside

the point. It is totally irrelevant to allocate 'blame'
between an incompetent or 'unpatriotic' management and a work force sufficiently cohesive and
organised to resist any changes which it sees as
against its short term interests. What matters is
the nature of the problem. This has less to do
with mobilising and diverting resources which
are currently untapped or misused, and much
more to do with the management and control of
resources. British industry has been caught between
two mutually conditioning forces: the complacency
and defensiveness of its capitalist class and the
power of resistance of its working class. This state
of reciprocal siege in a social and ideological
context which was becoming less dominated by
capitalist norms, increasingly emasculated the
dynamic capacity of British capital. In broad terms
the consequence is that only the working class can
take up the role of national leadership and assume
responsibility for industrial regeneration. The
situation into which the British economy has
drifted offers a major opportunity to link the
perspective of workers' control over the fundamental direction of the labour process with Britain's
central economic problem.

Planning Agreements

The natural institutional vehicle for realising this
perspective would be a comprehensive system of
planning agreements with leading private and
public companies. Under such a system company
plans and decisions about investment, technology,
manpower, overseas contracts, location policy and

so on, would become bound within the framework of socially determined objectives and stipulations. Its effectiveness in achieving economic, social and political advance would depend on four conditions. First, company agreements would need to be set within the framework of an overall plan for the development of national resources. Without a plan to provide sectoral targets and guidelines, industrial policy would be ad hoc and partial. The socialisation of enterprise planning is doomed to failure without government macro-planning, just as government macro-planning lacks social pressure without movement and involvement at enterprise and plant level. Demands and activities need to be paired both from bottom to top and from top to bottom.

Second, each planning agreement would need to be discussed and negotiated on the broadest possible multilateral basis, involving in addition to government and company representatives, union officials, shop stewards, local authorities, community bodies, environmental interests and so on. This would be important not only to build in a series of democratic checks and balances, but also to disseminate the experience of industrial decision-making, to challenge the idea that expertise is or should be the prerogative of a few and begin to make responsible self-government a reality.

Third, agreements would need to be backed by an element of compulsion. Without adequate sanctions against powerful recalcitrant companies, the whole exercise could become nullified. Sanctions might take a graduated form ranging from adverse publicity and withdrawal of financial inducements, tax concessions and government contracts, through discriminatory use of price controls to the ultimate threat of outright national-isation. Escalation from one stage to the next would at all times depend on the local, and some-times national, balance of social, ideological and political forces. In fact the struggle to win and implement a planning agreement is a microcosm of the whole project of gradualist social revolution.

Fourth, there would probably need to be a selective initial extension of public ownership along the lines laid down in the Labour Party's 1973 Programme which advocated that the state take over completely or acquire a major stake in at least one leading private company in each main industrial sector. The precise scale of public owner-ship required cannot be reduced to any simple formula but would depend on a process of mutual adjustment between the scope and time scale of the objectives aimed at, and the balance of forces at various levels of society. But the rationale of extended public ownership within a planning agreement system would be threefold: first, to improve the speed and realism of the planning process by providing the state and the public with inside information on which to assess the information supplied by the remaining private firms; second, to equip the state with a means of harnessing the forces of competition behind socially determined priorities and goals; third, to reinforce the effect of any sanctions threatened or imposed against non-compliant firms by establishing a ready made network of state owned companies into which rebels and miscreants could be absorbed.

It is abundantly clear that there is little prospect of any of these conditions being met under the present government or any immediately foreseeable governmental combination. But this does not mean that the whole concept of planning agreements should be quietly shelved to await a more favourable political conjuncture, when the old proposals can be retrieved, dusted off and held out as an instant solution to the economy's problems. The great virtue of the planning agreement idea is that it offers a mobilising potential which can be realised now. It does not require all energies to be polarised towards the next General Election or some fundamental shift in the patterns of political allegiance. The absence of the conditions necessary for the success of a system of planning agreements need not prevent either the labour movement or the newer social movements from pressing on with their own plant, enterprise, industry, locality or regional proposals for planning agreements, precisely in order to mobilise the social and political forces which could place the implentation of these proposals on the national political agenda.

The Politics of Hegemony

In this chapter we consider first what general implications can be drawn from the view of socialist strategy which we have outlined, for political action and the role of political parties. We then examine the specific structures of British politics and the factors which have shaped the political formation of the British left, paying particular attention to the nature of the Labour Party. Finally we explain in general terms what we see as the most feasible route by which the party political vehicle for a hegemonic socialist strategy can be created in Britain.

1. Political Power and Political Parties

Policies need political structures to be implemented. Some kind of organisational form is needed to create socialism. It goes without saying that the political structures implied by all we have written are complex and stretch across all forms of social activity. As they emerge and develop they will reflect the gradual growth of popular control in all areas of society. This statement, though simple, is necessary and important. For it embodies a view of political action, which runs counter to both the main left wing traditions of this country — the social democratic and the Marxist-Leninist.

We leave until later any detailed consideration of the two principal organised representatives of these traditions — the Labour Party and the Communist Party. For the moment what concerns us is that despite their incompatibility with respect to theoretical outlook, ultimate objectives and methods of attaining them, these two traditions have shared a common, highly restricted conception of political power and political action. For social democracy, Parliament and electoral activity focussed on Parliament are the sole legitimate ground of politics. Politics becomes that done by political parties. Underpinning this definition is the view that political power resides within elective institutions. Periodically, at election times, this power is momentarily dispersed amongst the citizens before it becomes reconstituted into a new unity. Hence the entire energies of the political party are polarised towards the supreme moment when power is dissolved and resolved. It is significant that the revolutionary extreme left has adopted a view of political power and action which is the mirror image of this. It dismisses Parliament as a facade or sham, but insists that power rests in the central core of the state apparatus which monopolises the legitimate use of coercion. The capture of this inner citadel by some sudden political or quasi-military manoeuvre organised by "the party" is the ultimate objective of political action, for which everything else is, in the end, considered preparatory.

Social democrats and such revolutionary Marxists may disagree as to the location of political power and hence as to the focus of political action. But they are at one in regarding political power as the exclusive preserve of a narrow range of institutions. It is this basic conception which we believe to be mistaken.

The society we have described is one in which power is widely diffused; capitalist dominance is maintained by a web of interlocking structures, including many not recognised as "political". As a result no simple meaning can be given to the phrase "taking power". It certainly cannot be reduced to winning elections on the one hand, or seizing control of the police, armed forces or mass media on the other. We have argued that socialist advance comes about by winning the diverse structures of power for socialism. This statement is necessarily imprecise because the meaning of socialism cannot be encapsulated in a single phrase. Nevertheless it is vital to recognise that political institutions exist in all areas of human activity. They may not be recognised as such because of the conventions of bourgeois politics. These conventions, which revolutionary groups often share, not only define what kinds of *actions* are proper, but also serve to organise certain *issues* out of the domain of politics altogether, so that some interests never even reach the agenda of public debate and action.

One of the great advances of the last decade has been the growth of awareness that political structures extend beyond the bounds of electoral politics. This advance is linked with the recognition of the role of bourgeois hegemony in maintaining the dominance of capitalism. The political practice of the left has only just begun to be influenced by this recognition. For the most part the left continues to organise as if simple physical repression combined with ideological manipulation through the mass media were the mainsprings of capitalist domination.

If this latter attitude is accepted it makes sense to define political power in terms of a single core of state institutions. If, however, domination is maintained by a wider and more subtle set of social, ideological and cultural controls then such a narrow focus can no longer be justified. It is precisely the Labour's Party's complicity – on the right by conviction, on the left by default – in restricting the arc of political action, which has disarmed successive Labour Governments. The mistake of Marxist critics has been to assume that the failures of Labour governments have arisen from an inability or unwillingness to grasp the levers of state power with sufficient firmness. The real failure has been one of which Marxists have also been guilty – the failure to see the importance of the struggle for hegemony and its implications for political practice.

Our view of political struggle implies that political institutions are formed wherever a struggle is waged over an area of social or individual control. The women's movement is political not because it 'politicises' women in the sense of channelling them towards other activity outside 'women's issues'; nor because it impinges on some other 'respectable' areas of political work as in trade unions; nor because it is supported by political parties. It is political in its own right because it directly confronts the structures of social control through which the oppression and subordination of women are perpetuated. No other legitimation is required.

This insistence on a wider definition of the political does not eliminate the need for political parties. It does, however, supply a perspective which is usually missing when the political is defined solely in terms of political parties. For whatever the party's original purpose, the view that political power resides in a single set of institutions inevitably transfers the burden of achieving change to the party. The correspondence between the party and the structures it wishes to control or replace is too clear-cut for it to be otherwise. This is true whether the party aims at gradual parliamentary change or at violent revolution. Political alliances become conceived as *party* alliances and party political activity takes the highest place in the scale of all political activity. And as all movements and struggles are constantly referred back to the political party, political activity outside the party will tend to be under-estimated and down-graded.

Both the social democratic and the Leninist left have tended to assume that the decisive advance towards socialism will consist of measures enacted by a revolutionary or radically reformist central government, whether constitutionally elected or otherwise. Now it is true that no programme of social transformation can be envisaged which bypasses the central institutions of the state. The achievement of state authority, the reconstitution of state institutions and the deployment of state power and resources remain indispensable aspects of the socialist project.

But to say that something is a necessary feature of socialist advance is not to assign it exclusive importance. The left's traditional pre-occupation with the apex of the pyramid of political power has had a paralysing effect on its thought and practice. It has induced a state of chronic long-sightedness which blocks or distorts the left's vision of the problems and possibilities of the present. Thus, in almost all discussions of socialist strategy, the participants tend to set their sights on some unspecified future breakthrough when the big prize of state power will already have been won or at least lie within grasp. Whilst it may conceivably serve some function of psychological motivation, this tendency to gaze into the political horizon and speculate about what lies beyond, produces constant confusion between imagination, aspiration and reality − between what could happen, what it is hoped might happen and what probably will happen.

Moreover, the habit of always living for some more or less remote future obscures the prospects for making gains in the present. If one assumes that permanent institutions of popular control can only begin to flourish after and as a consequence of some comprehensive, central government thrust, then opportunities for building such institutions here and now will be missed or given low priority. By contrast the broad perspective of political action and power which we are advocating here encourages an active search for openings and opportunities to promote the growth of responsible self-government and self-management in the workplace and the community. For within this perspective these developments, however small scale and limited, become the motive force for socialist change rather than its product.

2. The Functions of Political Parties

This perspective does not, as we have noted, eliminate the specific functions performed by political parties. For politics involves an orientation towards society as a whole. The political level of a social formation is that on which the relations between all social classes and forces converge. Effective political strategy therefore demands a perspective which is universal in its scope, which engages with or takes into account the needs, interests and aims of all diverse groups and forces. It is precisely the failure to acknowledge this which characterises all forms of economism.

One of the major functions of any socialist party is to co-ordinate, sustain and inform political action which originates outside itself. In practice a measure of such co-ordination will occur spontaneously. In part this is because the level of social militancy on some issues is governed by certain general feelings or tensions. Thus an upsurge of activity in one area over one set of issues will be accompanied by comparable upsurges elsewhere.

Geographic separation will also be broken down as people meet in the course of common action; and there is always an interchange of ideas and experience going on. But these processes are uneven and uncertain. It follows that a socialist party must identify and spread "best practice", forge connections and sometimes supply organisational staying power to ride out downturns in the level of activity. In the British context one of the most important aspects of this general function of co-ordination is to locate, communicate and enrich those objectives or themes which apparently diverse movements have in common. The left has only just begun to develop the links between industrial struggle and the various social movements concerned with issues of collective responsibility and control. The gap between these movements has hitherto been a major source of weakness for both.

This function would probably be readily accepted by all left political groups, though disagreements would remain about how it was to be interpreted. But it is the second general function of a socialist political party which is usually the focus of the strongest disagreement and acrimony on the left. At any given time the overall political situation in any country is characterised by a particular balance of forces. Some elements of this balance must be regarded for practical purposes as fixed: their tempo of change is too slow to be affected by any possible short run intervention. Other elements are more malleable and can be shifted in some desired direction by correctly judged intervention.

Any political party is continually called upon to respond to the current situation. But if, as we have noted, politics and government require a universalistic outlook, the responses made by an effective party will have to be framed within some set of judgements about the overall balance of forces, its prognosis and the prospects and consequences of various kinds of action.

Our discussion of incomes policy in the previous chapter illustrates the kinds of issues which are involved in formulating a response to a particular economic policy. In particular it shows how overall left advance or the blocking of advance by the right is likely to require voluntary restraint and sacrifice on one particular front of struggle. It is the specific task of a socialist party to make judgements of this kind, to define what it sees as the main political objective in any given situation, and, having done so, to publicise and argue for its position and seek to win popular conviction, even if, at times, this may mean temporarily swimming against the tide.

This function is of course always liable to degenerate into attempts at dictation or manipulation. Any appeal to the superior authority and wisdom of "the party", many examples of which exist in the history of both social democratic and communist parties, is automatically suspect. But despite this, and despite the more ludicrous manifestations of "party lines" among the left groups, any socialist politics must sooner or later come to terms with the need to assign priorities and lay down certain sequences and timetables.

Naturally the exercise of this function excites hostility amongst unaffiliated activists. It appears as arrogance and conceit, and this regardless of whether the party line is cautious or adventurist when measured against the scope, pace and intensity of development of social movements external to the party. And there is indeed a real tension involved. On the one hand, if the transition to socialism is conceived as a gradual process of developing hegemony over wider and wider areas of society, then "the party" can certainly be seen as working to accelerate and broaden this process. But it does so without asserting any primacy for party activity or insisting on any particular chronology. On the other hand, if the achievement of socialism depends on the outcome of particular critical events at the national political level, then a socialist party must of necessity opt for, seek to emphasise and win support for one particular line of development.

This problem cannot be resolved or lessened by introducing (or restoring) internal democratic checks and balances on the functioning of party leaderships, however desirable such reforms may be for other reasons. Nor is the problem a new one. The polemics by Rosa Luxemburg on the power of spontaneity and the unresolved conflict between the Bolshevik Party and the Soviets stemmed from much the same roots. However, whereas these early debates were perforce decided in favour of the party by the character of the times, the solution to the contemporary form of the problem is far less obvious. The source of the difficulty is that in the abstract both views of socialist transition cited above are correct. It involves both a gradual process of growth with an indefinite timescale, and the successful traverse of particular crises with quite definite durations and dimensions.

3. Political Parties and Social Movements

The easy way out of the tension between the organising and evaluative functions of political parties on the one hand, and the self activity of autonomous social forces on the other would be to refuse to choose and to rest content with the statement that both elements are needed. This is true. But it is an abstract, scholastic truth. It does not engage with the actual situation in which the British left finds itself. In our view the way out of the ghetto in which the left has become stuck lies in reversing the traditional social democratic and Leninist order of priorities between party politics and movement policies. Over the long run the tasks of building a series of mutually re-inforcing social movements around focal points of struggle with the common theme of democratisation, are more fundamental than winning and retaining Parliamentary power or building "the party". The perspective we have advanced contains a parliamentary and party political aspect, but subsumes it into a wider and richer vista of political change in the social practices through which society is organised.

a. The Leninist Party and Class Consciousness

At the risk of some repetition it is worth spelling

out the reasons for this emphasis. First it is fairly obvious that if a Leninist strategy for achieving socialism is outdated and inappropriate for advanced capitalism, the role of a socialist party inevitably becomes less absolute and overwhelming. This is true with respect to both the main tenets of the Leninist theory of the revolutionary party: its role in enabling the working class to transcend a mere trade union consciousness, and its role in the actual taking of state power. Only the former of these roles needs any further comment here.

The character and direction of working class struggle has changed to a degree which has altered the whole basis of working class consciousness. Both in terms of the industrial activities of trade unions, which spread across a wider and wider span of their members' lives, and in terms of inter-union activity over economic and social policy, the phrase "mere trade union consciousness" is no longer apt. Moreover, it is no longer correct to equate working class organisation with trade unions, even if the shop steward movement is simply classed as an adjunct to trade union activity.

Outside trade unions there has been an enormous expansion of working class organisation. Some of the developments are not directly political; others have been casually dismissed as middle class. What this dismissal ignores however is that activities embracing social, cultural, sporting and educational bodies, are part of a general pattern of social development in which far more people than before are becoming accustomed to the process of organisation and decision taking. Consider, for

..ple, the playgroup movement. This has
..olved thousands of mothers in collective action
and provides a direct link with problems of immense
social importance. The superficial simplicity of
this activity disguises the considerable degree of
social sophistication and responsibility, as well as
organisational competence which are required to
set up and run a playgroup. The fact that such
activities have no immediate 'political' function is
irrelevant.

The jibe that these activities are 'middle class'
ignores the fact that many of those so labelled
belong to just those 'new' working class groups
which have played such a central part in recent
years in extending the scope of trade union activity.
Either this latter phenomenon must also be dismissed as 'middle class' or the importance of
developments such as the women's movement and
environmental groups must be conceded. The dual
standard which, for example, admits well paid male
members of TASS as spearheads of working class
struggle, but rejects as 'middle class' their wives, or
even female members of the same union, when
they are active in an abortion campaign, illustrates
the confusion into which Marxist analysis has fallen.

Finally working class history and experience are
now sufficiently rich to be themselves an important
source of new ideas, methods of work and ways of
turning old ideas to new uses. Examples are the
flying pickets used by the miners in 1926 and re-
invented in 1972, and the factory occupation, used
in the 1930s abroad and applied with new force in
the 1970s in Britain.

Two examples illustrate the way in which the social conditions of advanced capitalism serve to produce a consciousness which transcends simple trade unionism. First, workers are now able to perceive, almost as a matter of course, the possibility that *they* could run a factory more effectively than their bosses. This perception is often only galvanised when an enterprise approaches bankruptcy, and usually does not extend beyond a single factory. But it is a major step forward.

A second example is that individual poverty caused by unemployment, illness or even fecklessness, is no longer seen as a matter solely for individual remedy. The widespread system of welfare payments, brought about by working class political pressure, has largely altered the way poverty is perceived. Those who mourn the passing of pre-war community spirit usually gloss over the fact that this spirit co-existed with a communal acceptance of individual poverty and a marked social passivity. An acceptance of general social responsibility to alleviate poverty may have paralleled a loss of 'neighbourliness' (though surely not caused it), but it is nonetheless a major social advance insofar as it automatically raises the question of collective responsibility and action.

b. The Priority of the Policies of Hegemony

It cannot be too strongly emphasised that the politics of hegemony are not to be equated with the winning of allies, whether socially in terms of the broad democratic alliance, or politically in terms of an alliance of political parties. What must

underpin any such alliance and is the only safe-
guard against the degeneration of hegemonic politics
into backroom deals and electoral manoeuvres, is a
firm commitment to the *policies* of hegemony and
the transformation of social practice.

Conversely this emphasis should serve to innocu-
late socialists against purist conceptions of alliances
based on little more than dogma, sentiment or
conceit. In principle there is no reason why, say,
sections of top management in public or private
corporations, or leading officials within the civil
service, or, for that matter, members of the police
and armed services, should be regarded as beyond
the pale of a progressive alliance around a particular
programme of policies.

Similarly a serious commitment to the social
movements which are the vehicles for changes in
social organisation, provides the key to realising
political unity on the left, notably between the
Communist Party and the Labour Party, which has
hitherto been either ignored or considered solely in
in terms of relations between organisations. This
issue will be taken up more fully later when we
have examined the particular form taken by left
disunity in Britain. But the general meaning
and importance of the claim asserted here, that
emphasis on movement politics can serve to
stabilise and redirect party political relations, is
conveyed by the final argument of this section.

It may be objected that the account given here
removes the emphasis on crisis, which in Leninist
politics is central, to a vague and unspecified
periphery. There are two reasons for this. The first,

a historical judgement, is that the most likely form of political crisis foreseeable in Britain will centre around an intensified electoral struggle. Such an electoral crisis falls within the capacity of existing party forms providing they have been informed by the kind of wider movement we have emphasised.

That this is only a judgement can be seen by the example of Ireland where political crisis has not developed in an electoral frame. Even so we maintain such a judgement for Britain. However, *even if* we are wrong, then we believe that the path of deepening genuine popular movement gives the only possible security against more authoritarian and non-electoral form of crisis. There seems to us no tenable position between this and the extreme that when armed resistance is necessary it will be too late to prepare for it. And that extreme has led, via the blood of a whole generation in Latin America, to the Stuttgart Stamheim prison and beyond.

c. Towards Left Renewal

The most obvious reason for stressing the primacy of social movements rather than political parties, is that a political party, or immediately realisable combination of parties, capable of following the strategy for socialism which we have outlined, does not exist. This fact is sufficiently indicated by our use of such unspecific phrases as "an effective socialist party".

It does not, however, follow that yet another attempt should be made to create this elusive animal. This conclusion almost invariably forms the culmination of Marxist political analysis. Political debate on the left tends to be conducted in terms of which of half a dozen aspiring socialist parties is best fitted for the role of revolutionary leadership. (It is a revealing paradox that Marxists tend to assume that the revolutionary party is, or will be when it exists, unique.) What in our view is wrong with this whole universe of discourse is that it remains trapped within the model of political action which sees "the party" as the final focus and directing agent for external movements.

Our argument is that social development and the strategic requirements for achieving socialism have outrun the capacity of the existing organisations of the left. The conclusion we draw is that work must be directed towards overcoming this maladjustment within all these organisations, especially the Labour Party, but also including the Communist Party and the more influential groups of the far left. The important point is to eliminate party conceit and to recognise the need for left renewal in Britain. The main themes which should inform this renewal can be summarised as follows.

1. Socialism is not a distant goal lying beyond the horizon but a reality which can be achieved here and now within an overall context of capitalism as a precondition for ending it.

2. The meaning of socialism must be demonstrated in practical ways in people's everyday lives, not confined to the phrases of political programmes.

3. The process of building socialism is a continuous one, which ebbs and flows, and in which no gain

is ever absolute and permanently guaranteed against loss.

4. The left must break with its oppositionist mentality and adopt a responsible and constructive approach towards issues of policy.

5. The scope of political action should be defined as broadly as possible both in terms of the social forces involved and in terms of the issues regarded as politically important.

6. Contemporary socialism requires a style of political work which is humbler, more tolerant, less strident and less Calvinistic that has historically been associated with the left.

4. The Structure of British Politics

We have set out some general principles and emphases which we believe can be used to renovate and revive socialist politics in Britain. It remains to consider the specific implications of our discussion for the parties of the left and the relations between them. Rather than detailing a complete inventory of the left, we have chosen to concentrate our analysis on the Labour Party. Part of the reason for this is the simple historical fact that the Labour Party has dominated British working class politics for the best party of this century. But also, as our argument makes clear, if one leaves aside the possible, but unlikely, scenario in which a period of repression by a right wing authoritarian government is brought to an end by a popular uprising, the only viable route to socialism in Britain lies through the Labour Party.

The structures of British politics are amongst the more enduring features of our society. Even now after a decade of almost uninterrupted economic crisis, including a period of major economic class struggles, which, for the first time in British politics led directly to the defeat of an incumbent government, these structures remain impressively robust. The signs are that those major constitutional changes which are now on the agenda of British politics — devolution, the introduction of proportional representation and the shift, heralded by the Lib-Lab pact, towards coalition government of the centre — can also be accommodated without the national trauma which accompanied the transition from the Fourth to the Fifth Republic in France, or the reconstruction of a viable governmental combination in Italy after the failure of the centre-left formula of the 1960s. Outside Scandinavia, Britain continues to be the most politically stable country in the West.

In all essentials Britain's political system remained unchanged for 50 years after 1924 when the Labour Party formed a minority government with the support of the Liberals. Since then governmental power has oscillated between the two major parties, sometimes with decisive parliamentary majorities, but seldom with actual majorities of those voting. These two parties have remained essentially the same and have suffered no major splits. The Ramsey MacDonald defection merely illustrated the durability of the Labour Party: only a handful of MPs and members followed him. As far as the Conservative Party is concerned, the split with the Ulster Unionists was no more than the consolidation of political changes frozen in 1914. Despite the very rapid growth of the National Front only the Scottish National Party can seriously claim to have significantly modified the dominant pattern of two party politics.

Internally both main parties have undergone a similar evolution. Their MPs have increasingly been drawn from the same social strata, eschewing on the one side, manual working class members recruited via the trade unions, and on the other the traditional gentry. The lecturer/marketing consultant MP is now the principal image of both sides. Their memberships have dropped, notably so as in the case of the Labour Party.

Outside the Labour Party, a small and politically isolated minority of Marxists – in 1924 mostly members of the Communist Party, now splintered into various groups – wield a certain sectional influence in the trade unions, but have virtually no electoral support. This minority carries a tradition of Marxist political theory which is almost entirely absent within the Labour Party. In fact the division of the British left between impotent theory and unguided power is almost complete.

The broad contours of the British left have been shaped by three major events. The first was the formation of the Labour Party by the Labour Representation Committee of the TUC. The unique attachment between the British Labour Party and the trade unions is well known both as a strength and as a weakness. Equally unique amongst European social democratic parties is the fact that this method of formation left the Labour Party with no self-conscious theory of power and very little clear-cut purpose beyond the defence of trade union rights. We explore the consequences of these formative features of the Labour Party in more detail below.

If this first event was peculiarly British the second originated in continental Europe. The fact that Britain became affected was an artificial consequence of a new found working class inter-nationalism. The great political schism of the 1920s, when the Communist Parties split away from their parent socialist parties, can be seen either as the inevitable consequence of the collapse of the Second International, or as a deliberate and necessary step to establish an autonomous working class revolutionary party, or as an unfortunate result of an enthusiastic and over ambitious Inter-national which led to a disastrous disunity of the left. Whatever one's general opinion about these events, the British episode in the drama took the form not of a principled and well-argued split, but rather of an arbitrary coalescence of a disparate collection of groups and individuals outside the main working class party.

Whether this division was historically justified is outside the scope of this review. What must be noted are its two main consequences. First, the Marxist tradition of political thought remained an isolated and essentially alien part of British politics. This is not to deny that individual Communists exercised influence, or that the Communist Party as a whole made some important interventions on certain issues. But in general this assessment stands.

The second result was rather more indirect. The major European splits were traumatic events that left their marks for many years. But their very magnitude, the fact that most members of the working class were forced to choose between competing strands of socialism, gave the question of political unity a mass significance.

It is no accident that even in modern Germany, where the Communist Party existed for many years in semi-clandestine form after being physically wiped out, and where its current support is very small, the question of joint action with the Communists is raised as a serious issue by the left of the German Social Democrats. In France, Italy and Spain, the matter is of course, of crucial significance. Yet the issue is not even touched upon within the British Labour Party.

The problem in Britain is not so much one of the comparative size of the Labour Party and the Communist Party or the groups of the far left. Rather it is that the issue of political unity has never been given any serious mass face. It is not so much unresolved as unformulated. This does not mean that political unity is unimportant in Britain. It remains vital. But disunity amongst the various political formations and sectional movements which in a broad sense comprise the left is less of an open wound and more of a general infirmity.

The third formative event in the evolution of the left was the triumph of Stalinism, or more precisely the equation of socialism with Stalinist Russia. It is not in fact true that sympathy and solidarity with the Soviet Union were confined to the Communist Party. Such sentiments have been widespread in the Labour left. Nevertheless the total acquiescence of the Communist Party in Stalinism widened the gulf which divided it from both the Labour Party and the mass movement. It has also been the major cause of the splintering of the Marxist left in Britain over the last 20 years. Both these consequences of the Communist Party's identification with the Stalinist version of socialism have thus embedded disunity more deeply into the custom and practice of the left.

That even this final act in the formation of the British left was essentially completed 40 years ago emphasises the fact that British socialism follows the general pattern of British political institutions in its enduring stability. The problem is to find ways of disengaging from the grip of the past and of reshaping the left, which neither reduce to tactical organisational manoeuvring, nor take off into flights of fancy. To begin to solve this problem it is necessary to explain not simply why the Labour Party came into existence, but why it has survived and flourished.

5. The Labour Party

That such a strange animal as the Labour Party cannot exist, and that its apparent reality is only a temporary and insubstantial shadow, is an assessment particularly common amongst Marxists. Accustomed to looking beyond political manipulation and *real politik* to some more fundamental dynamic, they have been persistently bemused by the apparent stability of the Labour Party in the face of repeated political betrayals. The Left/Right division has never quite boiled over into an actual split. The Labour Party has survived and continues to unite a loose and diverse coalition of political tendencies, unlike the Socialist Parties of Continental Europe which long alo split into two or three groups representing non-socialist reformers, reformist socialists and revolutionaries. In order to understand the unity and staying power of the Labour Party, it is necessary to explore the consequences of the fact that the Labour Party originated and has functioned as the political arm of the trade union movement, though of course this has not been the only role it has performed. The trade union link has been a source of strength in four important ways.

First it has determined the basic cleavage within the British political system as a *class* cleavage. The importance of this can be gauged by considering the United States where the organised working class never achieved significant, independent political representation; or Continental Europe where religious affiliation has been a major source of party differentiation; or Northern Ireland where the incompatible national identifications and aspirations of the Protestant and Catholic communities have defined the central political division.

Whatever the actions of Labour Governments, the basic attachment between the unions and the Labour Party has been difficult to evade over the long run. It was precisely the strains caused by incomes policy and the abortive trade union legislation of 1969 which led to the formation of the Labour Party-TUC Liaison Committee in 1972. This Committee was the architect of the Social Contract and of most of Labour's legislative programme when it resumed office in 1974. It also strongly influenced the decision of the Parliamentary Labour Party in electing Callaghan to succeed Wilson. The main qualification to this general assessment is that since the rise of political nationalism in Scotland, and to a lesser extent Wales, the simple class basis of the Labour Party has proved to be a source of conservatism and weakness.

Second, Labour's roots in the trade union movement have been an essential element in the internal stability which has characterised the Party's history. Thus even in the darkest hour of 1931, when MacDonald defected to lead a National Government dominated by the Conservatives, and when the Parliamentary Labour Party was decimated in the subsequent election, the Labour Party as a whole remained solid. This was undoubtedly because it was able to fall back on its familiar stance as defender of class interests, specifically against the bankers' ramp and the National Government, and in general against the whole capitalist system. At a crucial moment in its history the Party held together, and, though defeated, lived to fight another day.

Similarly other threatened splits and defections have never been consummated. The flirtation of figures such as Cripps and Laski with the Communist Party and Popular Frontism, petered out with the Nazi-Soviet pact and the outbreak of war. Right wing desertions, by Wyatt, Taverne, Mayhew, Prentice and Walden have been equally ineffectual, always restricted to a few, ambitious, maverick intellectuals. Almost certainly the enduring historical unity of the Party has been a major factor in the Tribune group's reluctance to engage in more than the minimal organisation implied by the existence of a Parliamentary group and a weekly newspaper. The power of the simple appeal to party loyalty has been repeatedly demonstrated in Labour Party history. And on the occasions when discipline has been used to deal with "parties within parties", as against the ILP in the 1930s, or against Trotskyist sects operating in the Party's youth wing, there has usually been little sympathy for the victims.

This historical solidity in turn has made it virtually impossible for the Communist Party or any other left group to outflank the Labour Party electorally. The CP's dismal electoral record over 60 years owes much to the fact that Labour's linkage with the trade union movement has entrenched it as *the* party of the working class. A voting system other than the first-past-the-post method could only have made a marginal difference to this state of affairs. Had the trade union movement been divided, or had the Labour Party lacked any mass trade union base, other left parties competing with Labour for electoral support, would have found at least the potential for growth. As it was, the only route for the CP to make its influence felt on national politics has in general run *through* the Labour Party via the trade unions, rather than in competition with it. The CP half admits this fact, but has never fully come to terms with it, preferring to nurse the illusion of an eventual electoral breakthrough.

The third positive result of Labour's institutional connection with the unions is that the Labour Party has always remained attached, though with considerable flexibility, to the objective of satisfying the most immediate needs and aspirations of its working class constituents and the institutional interests of the trade unions. Thus at the local level the Labour Party has correctly perceived the importance of local government as a source of advance in areas such as housing and education. At the national level from the 1906 Trades Dispute Act to the repeal of the Industrial Relations Act and the passing of the Employment Protection Act, the Labour Party has continued to fulfil its original function as the political instrument for the defence of the corporate interests of the trade unions. Always the most dangerous moment in the life of any Labour Government has been when it has been seen to depart too flagrantly from this function. At such times, as in the battle over "In Place of Strife", even the most hidebound trade union leaders have been willing to become temporary rebels.

Finally the Labour Party's base in the trade unions has forestalled the destiny repeatedly predicted to await it by Marxist critics: that it would become fully incorporated into the apparatus of bourgeois rule. As we argued in Chapter 3 it was the historic strength of the British trade union movement, particularly in the workplace, which blocked the attempt from 1964 to 1968 to overhaul and modernise British capitalism. The political aspect of this was on the one hand that establishment opinion which in 1964 had settled for the Labour Party as the political vehicle best fitted to carry through the modernisation process, became more pragmatic and ambivalent; whilst, on the other hand, the Labour Party itself was partially retrieved for its class purpose and began a major swing to the left which has still not wholly lost momentum.

The glaring and unresolved defect of the Labour Party, and particularly its left, has been its inability to develop a strategy for socialism based on anything other than the equation between power and electoral success. This weakness too can be traced back to the attachment between the Labour Party and the trade unions. The Labour Party was founded as the political counterpart of the trade unions' role as defenders of the corporate economic interests of the working class. In upholding the class interests of workers in Parliament the Labour Party was supposed to complement the work of the unions in industry. The conception was one of the trade unions and the Labour Party as equal partners in a common project. It is just this conception which is celebrated in the doctrine of the separation of industrial and political work.

This conception left the Labour Party without a clear theory of its political role beyond the simple defence of trade union rights. A wider purpose did eventually grow, as did a more articulate theory of political power and action. But the Party's initial amorphous state left it vulnerable to the natural pressures of the prevailing political system. These pressures moulded it into conformity with the restricted forms of political action which we analysed in the first section of this chapter.

Right wing domination of the Labour Party has not primarily been due to oligarchic manipulation, though, as in any party, machine politics has played its part in perpetuating the established leadership. It owes much more to the continued political and ideological weakness of Labour's Left, and, beyond that, of the left outside the Labour Party. Historically the Labour Left has usually lacked any clear alternative to the policies, and more fundamentally, behind the policies, the conceptions of political action favoured by the Right. The CP and the far left have for their part had little success in developing a strategy which resides anywhere but the never-never land of a Bolshevik uprising.

Two strands run through the politics of the Labour left. One has been a rough hewn Marxism based, particularly before the war, on ideas derived from Marxists about the inevitability of capitalist crisis and collapse. Capitalism was regarded as a system governed by its own inexorable laws which determined that it would eventually quite literally break down. At this point a socialist system would be established in a clean break. The main consequence of such ideas is that they preclude any notion of interventionist policies designed to shift the balance of forces in a favourable direction.

Socialist political action becomes dichotomised between defensive, reactive, and therefore subordinate, struggles over immediate class interests on the one hand, and advocacy and propaganda for socialism on the other. The field is thus in practice left free for command of practical politics to rest with the Right.

Moreover this cataclysmic view of the transition to socialism has suffered loss of credibility over the post-war period in the face of advanced capitalism's obvious economic success. The left's failure to come to terms with the realities of advanced capitalism has seriously weakened its mass appeal, whatever gains may have been registered within the structures of the Labour Party. Whereas it could with some truth be said that in 1945 there was a solid core of several million citizens for whom capitalism was in some sense a discredited system, and who were committed to the idea of replacing it with a new social order, no such large disaffected minority exists today. The discontent which has erupted over the past decade has focussed not on perceived gross deficiencies in the functioning of capitalism, but on the problems caused by capitalism's mature success.

The other strand in the politics of the Labour left has been one of moralistic criticism of capitalist society. Historically this strand was represented by the ILP and has its antecedents in the tradition of radical Protestant dissent. It is a political trend which certainly expresses a deeply felt aspiration for a new social order. But its vision of socialist politics as an evangelical crusade offers no effective theory of political action. Once again therefore it plays into the hands of the Right.

The fervour of the left has no doubt played an important role in sustaining any kind of radical politics. The force of moral indignation and righteousness has equipped the left with a powerful source of motivation and faith. But it has also helped to insulate the left from reality: it has provided spiritual compensation for the vale of tears presided over by the Right.

Not that the right has always enjoyed a smooth tenure. The left has a very long record of victories over resolutions at the Labour Party Conference. But these victories have rarely led to any significant change in the Party's actual practice, though they may have served to limit the leadership's room for manoeuvre. The mythology of the left attributes this failure to persistent betrayal and sharp practice by the Right. But this is inherently implausible. The particular brand of reformism consistently pursued by successive Labour leaderships has been one of the dominant political forces in Britain for the past thirty years. It can hardly be reduced to the chicanery of career politicians. If offensives by the left had really been backed by numerous and powerful social forces no amount of rearguard action by the Right could have staved off an eventual retreat. Indeed glimpses of such shifts in the internal balance of the Labour Party have been obtained whenever the passion of the left has co-incided with an upsurge in working class militancy as in the period from 1972 to 1974. If these glimpses have been brief, and if over the long run the mass party has been the servant rather than the master of the Party in Parliament, the reason is that the left has been weak. At least some of this weakness must be attributed to the left's own shortcomings. Its arena of political activity has been bounded by the same blinkered vision of the political process as that of the Right; and its world view has prevented it from intervening in politics with practical ideas on policy which could stand comparison with establishment orthodoxy.

The one exception to this pattern in recent years has been the attempt, spearheaded by Benn, to develop a realistic alternative economic policy and to build popular involvement into the process of Government policy making around the themes of industrial democracy and planning agreements. Despite Benn's partial eclipse since 1975, and despite the deep suspicions aroused by the ambiguities at the heart of these policies amongst those accustomed to fighting on clearer issues, there are signs that sections of the Labour Left have begun to tackle their past weaknesses. The problem of credible policy alternatives is under examination, and appreciation is growing that the success of any alternative policy depends on forging connections with movements and struggles which lie outside the narrow circle of electoral activity and Labour Party in-fighting.

These developments have happened to co-incide with a very significant phase in the history of the British Communist Party. The CP has made the first hesitant moves towards the eventual severance of its Soviet connection. It has also, in the recent revision of its programme "The British Road to Socialism", somewhat awkwardly, but nevertheless deliberately, followed some of the paths pioneered by the major Western Communist Parties. These cautious, but real, steps have opened up a perspective for the British Left which did not exist before.

An opportunity has been created, but as yet no more than that, to begin to turn hegemonic politics from an idea into a material force, to end that divorce between Marxism and practical politics which has characterised the British Left for over fifty years. To the extent that the CP finally lays the Soviet bogey to rest, it can reduce some of the distance which has cut it off from the mainstream of working class politics, whilst at the same time undermining some of the raison d'être of the groups on the far left. To the extent that the Communist Party seriously develops and applies the main concepts in its programme — social transformation as a process, the perspective of building a broad democratic alliance, and the primary role of the struggle to win mass popular consent — it can help to reduce the distance between the new social movements concerned with collective responsibility and democratisation, and the Labour movement. This in turn can help those forces in the Labour Party who are seeking to win it for a new political role which leaves behind both Parliamentary fetishism and the facile posturing of the ultra-left.

Such a process of re-assessment and re-orientation would of necessity have to be reciprocal. It cannot be seen as being masterminded by the Communist Party or any other political body. Nevertheless there are reasons for supposing that the CP has a crucial role to play if the process is ever to be set in motion. This is notwithstanding the CP's very real vices — its failures of internal democracy, its lingering allegiance to Moscow and the residue of sectarianism which is the obverse of its prolonged stigmatisation on the margins of political life. For all these defeats the CP carries a tradition of self-conscious Marxist theory and a habit and capacity for strategic political analysis, which is rare in the rest of the British left. It is almost certainly these characteristics, in conjunction with a new found openness both in internal debate and in external relations, which have made the Party attractive to what, in the British context, are quite significant numbers of intellectuals during the 1970s.

6. Conclusion

There are two possible political paths to socialism in Britain. The first involves a period of rightwing authoritarian government of indeterminate length, which would dissolve the political structures of the left in the corrosive acid of repression. The ousting of such a government, if and when it occurred, might allow the formation of a new alliance and a socialist government. That at least would be the hope.

This is a political scenario which many feel to be inevitable, even if not desirable. The unspoken sentiment behind a good deal of Marxist rhetoric is that things are going to get a lot worse before

they get better. It is suggested that the economic
problems of British capitalism must, sooner or
later, produce an authoritarian political reaction
in which the conservative right, probably with
army support, suspends all the processes of democracy, and, more or less crudely, destroys the
unions and the organised left.

This political perspective is the Siren of the
British Left. For whilst the dangers of a rightwing
takeover are continually brandished, and whilst
every action of the army or police is scrutinised
for its political implications, such a takeover has a
curious and seductive fascination. The Special
Patrol Group, Brigadier Kitson, army operations
at Heathrow, the involvement of the SAS in Ulster,
the imprisonment of building workers for picketing,
the calculated viciousness of the police at Grunwick
and Lewisham − all are used as demonstrations of
a political trend in the direction of an authoritarian
takeover. And not without some justification, for
there exists an influential group on the Right
which sees such a collapse of democracy as a
necessary part of national regeneration. Yet this
scenario is precisely that: an outline of a *possible*
political sequence. The trend which remains
dominant, and must therefore be given most
weight in any estimate of what is *probable,* is that
despite its stresses, Britain's political system
remains committed with surprising resilience to
the democratic process.

That the path to socialism may run through such
a period of repression cannot be entirely excluded.
What should be excluded is the tendency of groups

on the British Left to accept the inevitability of repression because it is the only path which justifies their existence. The Left is not without its own brand of mystical puritanism which hints that the working class will have to be purged of the sin of allegiance to social democracy by going through the purifying flame of repression. Then and, it seems, only then will they see their errors and accept the leadership of the true faith.

Many in the left groups would reject this portrayal, and it is, of course, a caricature. The problem is that the alternative path to socialism lies through the Labour Party. A third path, depending on a major switch in working class political allegiance away from the Labour Party and towards one or other of the Marxist groups within the framework of the present democracy, simply does not exist. This may be an unpalatable fact. Even those, like the British Communist Party, who have accepted it in principle, find it very difficult to realise in any practical shift in organisation.

Yet to say that the road to socialism, outside a period of physical repression, lies through the Labour Party does not of itself answer any of the political problems which confront those who would follow this road. The most important of these is that the Labour Party itself shows no historical tendency to move along such a path save in the most meandering and haphazard manner.

This is the unique and as yet unresolved problem of the British Left: the achievement of socialism by a party which historically has had no political sense of what socialism requires. The Marxist component of the British Left has for decades resisted coming to terms with this issue. It has preferred to follow one of two chimeras: that the Labour Party would split or lose mass working class support by pursuing reformist policies.

The general strategic issue is that of working class political unity. Its peculiarly British aspect is how to assert the need for unity in a context where left disunity has appeared as no more than an eccentric sideshow. The organisational tactics are too contingent to be considered here. There are however three basic considerations which must be invoked.

First the initiative has to be taken on the Marxist Left. Though there are capable Marxists within the ranks of the Labour Party, the Party collectively is neither theoretically nor practically equipped to deal with the strategic problem of working class unity unless the issue is forced from the outside. As we have already observed, whatever the rights and wrongs of those events that led to the present split in the left, the Communist Party has the potential to play a key role in uniting the left. To realise this potential, however, the Party will have to find the courage and humility to come to terms with much of its own history.

Second the question is not one which can be approached in a piecemeal, hole-in-the-corner fashion. Attempts to infiltrate non-Labour Party members on to the union delegations to Labour Party Conferences, will be seen, rightly, as organisational manoeuvres of undefined and suspicious intent.

Third, the problem is urgent and cannot be put off for yet another decade in the hope that the balance of forces will change, the Labour Party's right wing growing weaker and both the Labour left and the left outside the Labour Party growing stronger. Another turn of the wheel will not break the stalemate. It will simply embed the historical disunity more thoroughly in political psychology. The main positive impulse towards unity originating within the left, as opposed to general factors at work within society as a whole, is that a new generation of political activists is reaching maturity within both the Labour and the Marxist Left. This has brought about a cessation of the more merciless hostilities, which may yet fade if the normal state of left disunity is allowed to persist. The time is ripe for the left to solve its own problems. The danger is that if it does not, then its problems will be solved for it − but by extinction rather than expansion.